Atlas of Slavery

Atlas of Slavery

James Walvin

PEARSON
Longman

Harlow, England • London • New York • Boston • San Francisco • Toronto • Sydney • Singapore • Hong Kong
Tokyo • Seoul • Taipei • New Delhi • Cape Town • Madrid • Mexico City • Amsterdam • Munich • Paris • Milan

PEARSON EDUCATION LIMITED

Edinburgh Gate
Harlow CM20 2JE
United Kingdom
Tel: +44 (0)1279 623623
Fax: +44 (0)1279 431059
Website: www.pearsoned.co.uk

First edition published in Great Britain in 2006

ISBN-10: 0-582-43780-6
ISBN-13: 978-0-582-43780-7

British Library Cataloguing in Publication Data
A CIP catalogue record for this book can be obtained from the British Library

Library of Congress Cataloging in Publication Data
A CIP catalog record for this book can be obtained from the Library of Congress

10 9 8 7 6 5 4 3 2
09   08   07   06   05

Set by 35 in 9.5/12.5pt Stone Serif
Printed and bound in China
SWTC/02

The Publisher's policy is to use paper manufactured from sustainable forests.

Contents

Author's acknowledgements

This book would not have been possible without the initial prompting of Heather McCallum. She enthusiastically backed the idea, and sent me back to the drawing board when my first efforts were less than adequate. I owe her a great deal. John David Smith was also very supportive – though properly critical of many of the book's early shortcomings. His careful reading of my initial efforts enabled me to improve this book immeasurably. I am also indebted to the anonymous readers whose reports were thorough and constructive. The idea behind this book emerged from early discussions with Paul Lovejoy and I hope he recognizes his influence in what has found its way into print. For years I have talked about slavery with Gad Heuman and he too has influenced this book, often in ways he would not recognize. My agent Charles Walker has been a steadfast promoter of my interests and ideas, and I am, once again, immensely grateful to him. Two libraries proved invaluable: the Rockefeller Library of Colonial Williamsburg and the Jefferson's Studies Center Library at Kenwood, Monticello. James Horn and Andrew O'Shaughnessy kindly invited me to both places, and both went out of their way to make my visits enjoyable and productive. I completed this book at the Institute for Advanced Studies at La Trobe University and am immensely grateful to Gilah Leder and her staff for inviting me and ensuring that I had a productive stay. Alex and Ria Tyrrell, and Rhys and Colleen Isaac took care to ensure that we made the most of Melbourne when the library was closed. At Pearson, the staff led by Benjamin Roberts worked hard to transform my crude attempts to be a cartographer into a polished set of maps. My greatest debt is to my fellow historians, some of them named in this book (and especially my friends in the Association of Caribbean Historians) who continue to educate me about the complex history of slavery.

James Walvin

Publisher's acknowledgements

We are grateful to the following for permission to reproduce copyright material:

Map 1 redrawn from *The Ancient World: A Social and Cultural History, 2nd Edition*, reprinted by permission of Pearson Education, Inc. (Boren, H. C. 1986); Map 2 redrawn from *The Evolution of the Medieval World, 312–1500*, reprinted by permission of Pearson Education Ltd. (Nicholas, D. 1992); Map 3 redrawn from *A History of the Vikings*, reprinted by permission of Oxford University Press (Jones, G. 1968); Map 9 redrawn from *A World History, 3rd Edition*, reprinted by permission of Oxford University Press, Inc. and the author (McNeill, W. H. 1979); Maps 10 and 20 redrawn from *African History*, reprinted by permission of Pearson Education Ltd. (Curtin, P. D. *et al.* 1995); Map 11 redrawn from *Europe: A History*, pub Oxford University Press, Inc. and Pimlico, reprinted by permission of Oxford University Press, Inc. and The Random House Group Ltd. (Davies, N. 1993); Maps 15, 17 and 37 redrawn from *Slavery from Roman Times to the Early Atlantic Slave Trade*, pub University of Minnesota Press, reprinted by permission of the author (Phillips, W. D. 1985); Map 16 redrawn from *Transformations in Slavery: A History of Slavery in Africa*, reprinted by permission of Cambridge University Press (Lovejoy, P. E. 1983); Maps 19, 22, 46, 52 and 56 redrawn from Philip D. Curtin, *The Rise and Fall of the Plantation Complex: Essays in Atlantic History, 1st Edition*, Copyright Cambridge University Press 1990, Cambridge University Press, with permission of the author and publisher (Curtin, P. D. 1990); Map 21 redrawn from *A Social History of Black Slaves and Freedmen in Portugal, 1441–1555*, reprinted by permission of Cambridge University Press (Saunders, A. 1982); Maps 24, 25, 27, 28, 30, 44 and 67 redrawn from *Atlas of British Overseas Expansion*, reprinted by permission of Routledge (Porter, A. ed. 1991); Map 26 redrawn from *The Oxford History of the British Empire: Volume II: The Eighteenth Century*, reprinted by permission of Oxford University Press (Marshall, P. J. ed. 1998); Map 29 redrawn from *Shipping, Maritime Trade and the Economic Development of Colonial North America*, reprinted by permission of Cambridge University Press (Shepherd, J. F. and Walton, G. M. 1972); Map 32 redrawn from *African History*, reprinted by permission of Pearson Education Ltd. (Curtin, P. D. *et al.* 1978); Maps 33, 72 and 73 redrawn from *Dictionary of Afro-American Slavery*, pub Praeger, reprinted by permission of Greenwood Publishing Group, Inc. (Miller, R. M. and Smith, J. D. eds 1988); Map 34 adapted from *The English Atlantic, 1675–1740: An Exploration of Communication and Community*, reprinted by permission of Oxford University Press, Inc. (Steele, I. K. 1986); Map 35 redrawn from *The Shaping of America: a geographical perspective on 500 years of history. Volume I: Atlantic America, 1492–1800*, reprinted by permission of Yale University Press (Meinig, D. W. 1986); Map 36 redrawn from *The Atlantic World in the Age of Empire*, reprinted by permission of Houghton Mifflin Company (Benjamin, T. *et al.* 2001); Map 38 redrawn from *Way of Death*, reprinted by permission of The University of Wisconsin Press (Miller, J. C. 1988); Map 40 adapted from *Africans:*

The History of a Continent, reprinted by permission of Cambridge University Press (Iliffe, J. 1995); Maps 41 and 42 redrawn from *The Atlantic Slave Trade*, reprinted by permission of Cambridge University Press (Klein, H. S. 1999); Map 43 data from *The Atlantic Slave Trade*, reprinted by permission of Cambridge University Press (Klein, H. S. 1999); Map 45 redrawn from *Human Cargoes*, pub University of Illinois Press, reprinted by permission of the author (Palmer, C. 1981); Map 47 redrawn from *The Dutch in the Americas, 1600–1800*, pub John Carter Brown Library, © International Mapping, reprinted by permission of International Mapping (Klooster, W. 1997); Maps 48 and 55 redrawn from *A Brief History of the Caribbean: From the Arawak and the Carib to the Present*, pub Meridian Books, reprinted with permission of Facts on File, Inc. (Rogozinski, J. 1994); Map 49 redrawn from *The Routledge Atlas of African American History*, reprinted by permission of Routledge/Taylor & Francis Books, Inc. (Earle, J. 2000); Maps 50 and 51 redrawn from *Sugar Plantations in the Formation of Brazilian Society: Bahia, 1550–1835*, reprinted by permission of Cambridge University Press (Schwartz, S. B. 1985); Maps 53 and 54 redrawn from *The Portuguese Empire, 1415–1808: A World on the Move*, pub The Johns Hopkins University Press, reprinted by permission of the author (Russell-Wood, A. J. R. 1998); Map 57 redrawn from *Sugar Island Slavery in the Age of Enlightenment*, reprinted by permission of Princeton University Press (Stinchcombe, A. L. 1995); Map 62 redrawn from *The Oxford History of the British Empire: Volume I: The Origins of Empire: British Overseas Enterprise to the Close of the Seventeenth Century*, reprinted by permission of Oxford University Press (Canny, N. ed. 1998); Map 63 redrawn from *Tobacco and Slaves: The Development of Southern Cultures in the Chesapeake, 1680–1800*, reprinted by permission of The University of North Carolina Press (Kulikoff, A. 1986); Map 65 redrawn from *Encyclopedia of the North American Colonies*, pub Charles Scribner's Sons, reprinted by permission of The Gale Group (Cooke, J. E. ed. 1994); Map 66 redrawn from *Atlas of American History, 3rd Edition*, reprinted with permission of Facts on File, Inc. (Ferrell, R. H. and Natkiel, R. 1993); Map 68 redrawn from *Black Majority*, reprinted by permission of Alfred A. Knopf, a division of Random House, Inc. (Wood, P. H. 1974); Map 71 redrawn from *Speculators and Slaves*, reprinted by permission of The University of Wisconsin Press (Tadman, M. 1989); Maps 74 and 75 redrawn from *The Routledge Historical Atlas of the American South*, reprinted by permission of Routledge/Taylor & Francis, Inc. (Frank, A. K. 1999); Map 76 redrawn from *Chronology of World Slavery*, reprinted by permission of ABC-CLIO (Rodriguez, J. P. 1999); Map 77 adapted from *The Abolition of the Atlantic Slave Trade*, reprinted by permission of The University of Wisconsin Press (Eltis, D. and Walvin, J. eds 1981); Maps 79 and 81 adapted from *A Brief History of the Caribbean: From the Arawak and the Carib to the Present*, pub Meridian Books, reprinted with permission of Facts on File, Inc. (Rogozinski, J. 1994); Map 80 adapted from *Sugar Plantations in the Formation of Brazilian Society: Bahia, 1550–1835*, reprinted by permission of Cambridge University Press (Schwartz, S. B. 1985); Map 84 redrawn from *The Economy of the Indian Ocean Slave Trade*, reprinted by permission of Frank Cass, part of the Taylor & Francis Group (Clarence-Smith, W. G. ed. 1989); Map 85 redrawn from *The Nation Killers: The Soviet Deportation of Nationalities*, pub Macmillan, reprinted by permission of Palgrave Macmillan (Conquest, R. 1966); Map 86 redrawn from *Gulag: A History of the Soviet Camps*, first published USA by Random House, Inc., first published in Great Britain by Allen Lane 2003, Penguin Books 2004, reprinted by permission of Doubleday, a division of Random House, Inc. and Penguin Books Ltd. (Applebaum, A. 2003, 2004); Map 87 redrawn from *Recent History Atlas: 1870 to the Present Day*, pub in the UK by Weidenfeld, reprinted by permission of Routledge and the author (Gilbert, M. 1966).

In some instances we have been unable to trace the owners of copyright material, and we would appreciate any information that would enable us to do so.

List of maps

Preface

The history of slavery has attracted remarkable academic and popular attention in recent years, much of which has concentrated on the form of slavery – African slavery – that European settlers introduced into the Americas. Indeed, popular images of 'slavery' tend to involve Atlantic slave ships and slaves toiling on plantations in the Americas. Yet slavery existed long before the first Africans were shipped into the Americas, and it survived long after the West turned against slavery and sought to end it worldwide. Indeed, slavery thrives today in a number of societies. Anti-Slavery International (the descendant of the British Anti-Slavery Society, founded in 1823) is permanently busy tackling various forms of contemporary slavery around the world. The great optimism of nineteenth-century abolitionists, especially in Britain and the USA, that the world would be rid of slavery for ever, has simply not happened. In fact, in the mid-twentieth century, there may have been more slaves on earth than ever before. The millions of people ensnared by tyrannical regimes, notably Nazi Germany and Stalin's Russia, seem to have greatly surpassed the numbers of any known earlier slave system.

However, slavery in the Americas was very distinctive. It had a number of peculiar features. For a start, and unlike earlier slave systems, it became a highly *racialized* form of slavery. It also had an unparalleled geographical reach, involving three continents – Europe, Africa and the Americas. All this evolved over an enormous period of time (from the fifteenth to the late nineteenth century). At the same time, though perhaps more difficult to calculate, this system of Atlantic slavery brought great material well-being to the West but spread impoverishment and misery throughout Africa. It is, quite simply, an extraordinary story, and one that becomes more extraordinary the more we know about it.

This book is concerned primarily with slavery in the Americas but in the context of a broader account of earlier and later forms of slavery. But I am also trying to explain that history through a collection of maps and related text. The maps concentrate on particular themes in the history of slavery, but they are organized in the form of a narrative sequence. The aim is to illustrate the key features of the history of slavery in their defining geographical setting. After all, the African's enslavement, transportation, resettlement and lifetime of bondage were all determined by geographical experiences. Africans were transported huge distances, across land and water, through different climatic zones and physical experiences. Even their homes and workplaces in the Americas were determined by geography: they worked overwhelmingly in export crops, which were themselves shaped by topography and climate, notably in the tropics and subtropics. What follows is above all an attempt to illustrate the historical geography of slavery: to show how the peoples of three widely separated continents were brought together, through slavery, into an economic and human system that was, at once, grotesquely violent and cruel yet lucrative to those who owned and managed the system.

Maps alone cannot explain the full detail of that history, and the accompanying text seeks to explain the finer points of the historical account, but the two, text and maps, go together. It is a book that could not have been written without the efforts of other historians. My main challenge has been to render the complex findings of others into an atlas that explains a complicated history through both the written word and associated maps. I hope that what follows is both accessible for a range of readers and yet true to the scholarship of other historians.

Introduction

The enslavement of Africans and their transportation across the Atlantic has come to occupy a distinct, even a unique, place in the public imagination. Even at the end of the twentieth century, which was characterized by its own catalogue of horrors (including massive slave systems in Nazi Europe and the Russian Gulag), the Atlantic slave system continues to exercise a horrible fascination. Partly cultivated by popular culture, the 'Middle Passage' (the oceanic leg of that complex process of enslavement) is often assumed to represent slavery itself: cargoes of Africans packed below decks, for months on end, in conditions of stable-like filth, pitching their way towards the plantations of the Americas. In fact, this oceanic experience was only one element in a tortuous and protracted system that took Africans from their homelands to the very edges of the American frontier. Nonetheless, the European and American slave ships represent slavery at its most brutal and inhuman.

Slavery in the Atlantic world involved much more than the Atlantic crossing. It brought together three continents (Europe, Africa and the Americas) into an economic and social interdependence that was lubricated by the sweat of African slaves. It was a brutal system that lasted more than four centuries and that counted its victims (the dead and the damaged) in their millions. It is no accident that comparisons are frequently made between Atlantic slavery and the European Holocaust of the twentieth century. Indeed, the phrase 'African Holocaust' is often used (inappropriately) to describe the Atlantic system, but it is a misleading phrase. For all its violence and damage, the Atlantic slave system was *not* genocidal in intent or practice. However we choose to describe it, few serious scholars now doubt the centrality of this massive enforced movement of peoples across the Atlantic for the development of the modern Western world.

Atlantic slavery transformed the history of Africa, of the Americas and, less visibly and obviously, of Europe itself. Africa provided the labour so eagerly bought by Europeans on the African coast over a period of four centuries. From among the survivors of the slave ships (many of whom were sick when landed in the Americas), there emerged new black communities across the face of the Americas. They were, at first, communities of *slaves*. Black slavery differed from one part of the Americas to another, but wherever it took root, it became a seminal force in the shaping of the modern Americas. Moreover, not until the 1820s, when Europeans began to flee European poverty in large numbers, did the number of white migrants to the Americas begin to outnumber the imported Africans. Until then, the African was the key pioneer across swathes of the Americas.

From the first, Africans were shipped across the Atlantic primarily to cultivate export crops in tropical and subtropical regions. Most were destined to work in sugar, but armies of slaves also worked in tobacco, rice, coffee, indigo and a range of other commodities. In the USA in the nineteenth century, slaves were moved westwards from the eastern states to cultivate cotton in the new territories of the South and on the frontier. In what proved to be the last phase of slavery in the Americas, slaves in Cuba and Brazil were worked on new tobacco and coffee plantations in the last quarter of the nineteenth century.

From the early days of Brazilian sugar in the late sixteenth century, through to Southern slave-grown cotton in the mid-nineteenth century, all the major slave-grown crops were export crops. And from first to last Europe was central to the whole enterprise: from the pioneering settlements of the slave colonies, to the financial and political management of the slave settlements, as shippers, or as *entrepôt* for slave-grown products, Europe was a steadfast ally and beneficiary of the Atlantic slave system.

Though not always obvious or visible, Europe was the engine behind the development of African slavery in the Atlantic. Europeans were the guiding force behind the origins, development and perfection of the use of African slaves in the Americas. That much is obvious and indisputable. But why did Europeans turn to *Africa* for labour for their new settlements on the far side of the Atlantic? Why turn to Africans (not Europeans or indigenous peoples) for labour? And why did they use Africans *as slaves*, rather than other forms of labour? In the very years that Europeans began to use Africans as slaves, and began to ship them, in small but growing numbers, they were turning their back on slavery in Europe itself. Though they felt no qualms about using other forms of unfree labour in their American colonies (indentured labour or prisoners, for example), Europeans had effectively lost their appetite for slavery – at least the slavery of other Europeans. However, they seemed to have no worries about buying Africans as slaves, and whatever qualms they may have had in the early days of Atlantic slavery, their reservations were quickly overcome by the obvious effectiveness (and profitability) of using African slaves. To put the matter simply, African slavery worked: it provided labour, at a price Europeans could afford, in numbers they required, and all to profitable economic use. Thus it was that Africans were quickly reduced from humanity to inanimate objects of trade and economic calculation.

Europeans bought their African captives from other Africans. Though the first European maritime slave traders prowling the West African coast simply grabbed Africans whenever they could, this quickly gave way to a more settled, more formal system of trading, for humanity as well as other valued commodities. But for this, Europeans needed African traders and middlemen. All the goods transferred to Europeans on the coast passed through African hands, and that included growing numbers of African slaves, arriving on the coast from ever more distant regions of the interior. Though the transfer of Africans to the European slave ships was coastal, the origins of those slaves were increasingly remote and unknown (even to the African traders on the coast.) From this simple early system, enormously complex trading systems developed that reached deep into Africa and which ensured that millions of Africans were passed from hand to hand, from one internal African trading system to another, until finally the victims were delivered to the Europeans or their representatives on the coast. There they were eventually loaded into slave ships destined for the Americas – if they survived.

This trading system in African humanity reached its height in the late eighteenth century (when the British dominated the Atlantic trade). In the 1790s alone, British vessels shipped one-third of a million Africans across the Atlantic; a century earlier it had been 91,800. At its height, this trading system was vast, stretching along much of the African coastline, from Senegambia to Angola, around the Cape of Good Hope to Mozambique and reaching into the interior regions of Africa, about which Europeans knew little. It was to overcome this ignorance that in 1788 Sir Joseph Banks formed the *Association for Promoting the Discovery of the Interior Part of Africa*. There was also a thriving trade in Africans from the East African coast, feeding the voracious appetite for slaves in Arabia, the islands of the Indian Ocean and even as far away as India. Again, none of this could have been possible without internal African slaving systems. But that bald statement can deceive.

Did Europeans on the coast merely tap into those African systems, or did their insatiable appetite for slaves *cause* the development and growth of African slave systems (with all the consequent violent disruption)? Here we confront what has become one of those sensitive issues that distinguishes the history of Atlantic slavery. What forms did African slavery take *before* Europeans arrived on the coast? Were Africa's internal slave systems similar to those that evolved in the Americas? Or were they so thoroughly distorted by the demands of European slave traders that African slavery became something quite different? Behind these and a myriad other questions there lies the basic issue of African complicity in the story of Atlantic slavery. Could slavery in the Americas have thrived as it did without the help of African traders and African slavery?

It is at this point that we need to confront the role of Islam. Europeans had been familiar with African slaves in the Mediterranean long before the development of the Americas. For centuries, Islamic overland slave systems had delivered Africans to the slave markets of southern Europe and the eastern Mediterranean (and elsewhere). Indeed, it was the very existence of Islamic slave routes *within* Africa that first alerted Europeans to the possibilities of acquiring and developing their own slave-trading systems on the West African coast in the late fifteenth century. That early European slaving presence was a spasmodic, haphazard affair, but it took its cue from forms of slavery already existing on the coast and in the interior.

The European encroachment into Africa in the fifteenth and sixteenth centuries, though physically limited to restricted spots on the coastline and river systems, was part of a much broader European involvement with the wider world. Successive European maritime powers (in turn, the Spanish, Portuguese and Dutch) began to divide the globe into their own spheres of trading or colonial interest, governing, trading and overawing local peoples (where they could), shifting them around when necessary, and all for the promotion of European power and the enhancement of European material well-being. Wherever they travelled Europeans encountered social systems that they considered to be slavery. Of course, the various slave systems that they encountered around the world were *not* the same as the slave systems that emerged in the Atlantic economy, but as slavery became ever more important to the European role in Africa and in the Americas, Europeans became conscious of slavery as a worldwide phenomenon. In large part Europeans used local slavery, though often modifying it to suit their own broader purposes. For example, Europeans transformed existing forms of slavery in parts of West Africa into the massive flow of captives destined for the slave ships and the American plantations. But it was a system that evolved over a very long period, in conjunction with the European settlement of lands in the Americas. The Atlantic slave system thus emerged from the peculiar combination of American land, European money and management, and African labour.

All the major European maritime and colonial powers became embroiled with slavery to varying degrees. Yet, in a political and economic *volte-face* of staggering dimensions, they all eventually turned against slavery. Having spent the best part of four centuries as slave traders and proponents of slavery, for much of the nineteenth century Europeans campaigned *against* slavery around the world. However, this later abolitionist phase ought not to mask a simple fact, namely that from the fifteenth century (when Europeans first dabbled in slavery on the African coast) through to the nineteenth century, when they – especially the British – transformed themselves into fierce abolitionists, Europeans were deeply involved with slavery. They adopted it, modified it and transformed it to suit their interests. They shipped millions of people vast distances to work as slaves, they tapped into slave systems around the world and then, led by the crusading British, they resolved that the world should be free of slavery. The very system (or more accurately systems) that imperial Europeans had regarded, in the seventeenth and eighteenth centuries, as vital, by the nineteenth century they viewed as immoral and uneconomic. But from beginning to end, both as practitioners of the dark arts of slavery and as blustering abolitionists, maritime Europeans were deeply involved with slavery.

They were not alone; nor were they the first (or the last). Forms of slavery had been commonplace throughout recorded history and had been a generally unquestioned institution in any number of earlier civilizations, most notably perhaps in the world of classical antiquity. Medieval Europe had similarly been characterized by various forms of unfree labour. There was nothing new about societies using, relying on or creating labour systems that denied freedom to the labouring masses (or even to more refined social groups). In many of those slave systems, slavery was sustained by supplies of unfree labour from distant regions. Slave systems often depended on the enforced movement of armies of people from one region to another: in ancient Greece (Map 1), throughout the Roman Empire (Map 2), the Viking world of northern Europe (Map 3), in the expanding world of Islam (Map 4) and in pre- and early colonial Africa (Map 5) and Asia (Map 6). When Europeans first turned to African slaves, they seemed to be merely the latest in an ancient tradition of slavery and slave trading. However, these earlier slave systems were quite different from what emerged in the Atlantic world. What Europeans created in the enslaved Americas was utterly distinctive in scale, impact and consequence. There was, quite simply, nothing like Atlantic slavery in the earlier annals of slavery.

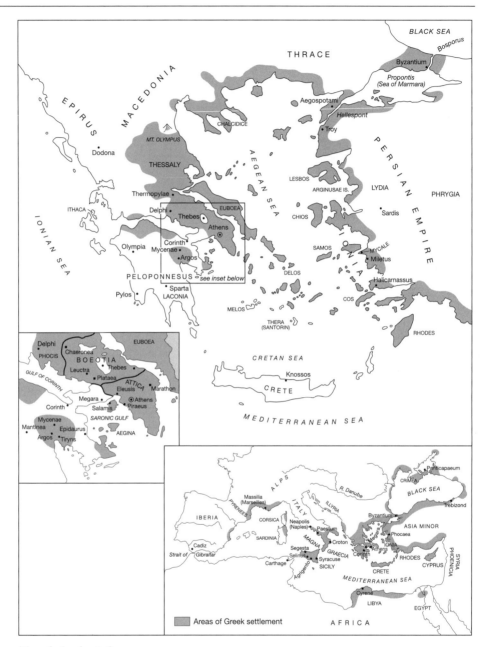

Map 1 Ancient Greece

Source: Boren, Henry C., *Ancient World, The: A Social and Cultural History, 2nd Edition.* © 1986.
Reprinted by permission of Pearson Education, Inc., Upper Saddle River, NJ.

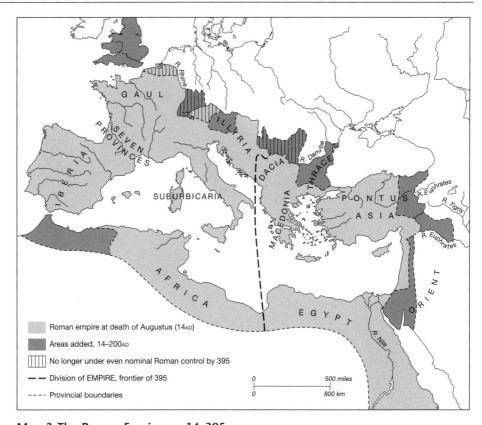

Map key:

- Roman empire at death of Augustus (14AD)
- Areas added, 14–200AD
- No longer under even nominal Roman control by 395
- Division of EMPIRE, frontier of 395
- Provincial boundaries

0   500 miles
0   800 km

Map 2 The Roman Empire, AD 14–395

Source: After Nicholas, D. (1992) *The Evolution of the Medieval World, 312–1500*, Longman, pp. 502–3.

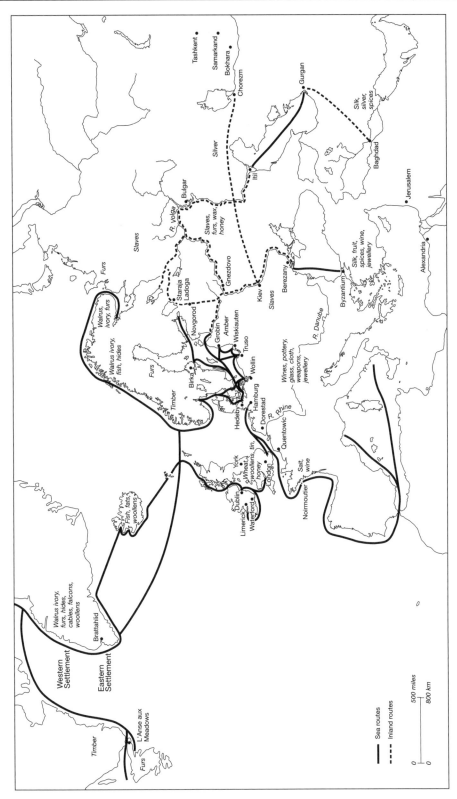

Map 3 European slave-trading routes in the era of the Vikings
Source: After Jones, G. (1968) *A History of the Vikings*, pp. 160–61. By permission of Oxford University Press.

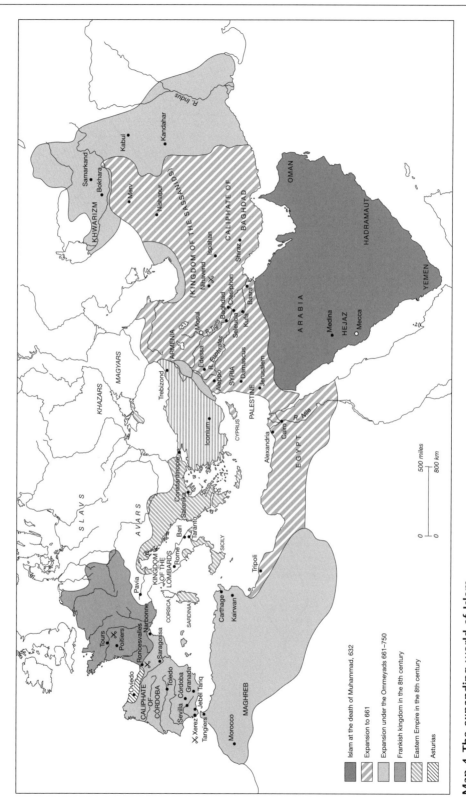

Map 4 The expanding world of Islam

Source: After de Vries, S., Luykx, T. and Henderson, W. O. (1965) *An Atlas of World History*, Nelson, Map 19.

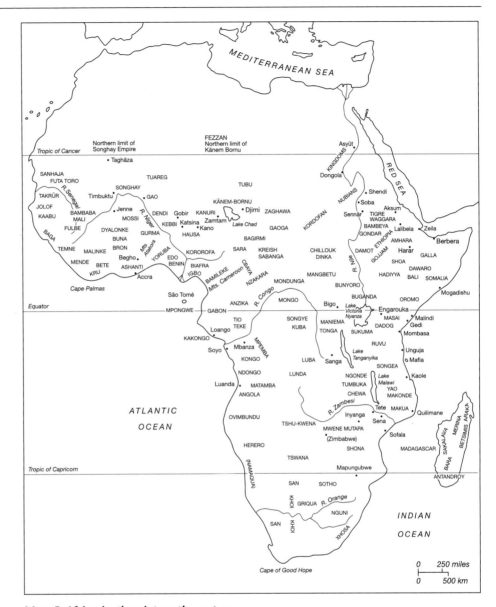

Map 5 Africa in the sixteenth century

Source: After Diop-Maes, L. M. (1993) *ANKH*, in Burke, P. and Inalcik, H. (eds) (1999) *History of Humanity: Scientific and Cultural Development: From the 16th to the 18th Century*, Routledge, p. 414.

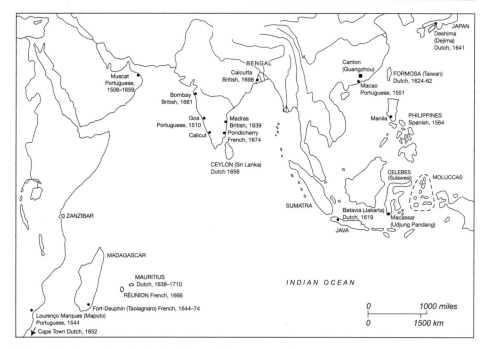

Map 6 Trade and colonies in sixteenth-century Asia

Source: After De Vries, J. (1975), in Burke, P. and Inalcik, H. (eds) (1999) *History of Humanity: Scientific and Cultural Development: From the 16th to the 18th Century*, Routledge, p. 129.

CHAPTER 1

Slavery in a global setting

The modern interest in Atlantic slavery and the African slave trade has, to a marked degree, overshadowed the study of slave systems in other parts of the world. When people speak of 'slavery' today they are likely to think of black slavery, and the slave system of the Americas. Yet American slavery is relatively recent, and in many respects unusual.

Wherever we look, slave systems dot (and sometime dominate) the historical geography of very different regions of the globe. From Indonesia to India, from South Pacific islands to Arabia, slavery was an unquestioned institution. So too was the supply of slaves (slave trades) to those regions, often from distant communities. Put simply, slavery and slaves were ubiquitous. Not surprisingly, then, wherever Europeans travelled in that age of maritime exploration beginning in the fifteenth century, they encountered slave systems. Perhaps the most important was the world of Islam.

Europeans had long been familiar with the slaves of the Islamic world: from its earliest days Islam was associated with slavery. Muhammad owned slaves, the Qur'an makes frequent mention of slaves, and there was a flourishing debate about slavery among Islamic scholars. As Islam spread, slavery travelled in its wake, and slave routes evolved to supply the demand for slaves in a host of Islamic slave societies. Sub-Saharan Africa proved a rich and long-lasting source of slaves for the world of Islam. From the eighth to the twentieth century large numbers of slaves were moved, mainly by foot, across the Sahara to Islamic slave markets dotted around the Mediterranean. Most of those slaves were black Africans from sub-Saharan Africa, destined to be sold and settled in the Arab Mediterranean. Many inevitably perished *en route*, while others were settled as slaves *within* the Sahara. Some even found their way to mainland Europe, appearing for example in a number of late medieval and early modern paintings. Though many African slaves were men, wanted as soldiers or for heavy manual labour in mines or agriculture, the majority were women to be used as servants or concubines. The numbers involved are difficult to calculate, but they seem to have increased markedly in the eighteenth and nineteenth centuries, prompted by economic growth in the Mediterranean and by aggressive slave trading in Africa itself.

Most of those slaves were captured violently in raids and then sold on to merchants or the overland caravans. It was, in addition, amazingly long-lived, surviving some twelve centuries. The most eminent scholar of the subject calculates that perhaps three and half million to four million slaves were transported across the Sahara in that period. It was, in Ralph Austen's words, 'one of the major examples of enslavement in world history'. It was variants of this *existing* internal African slave trade – overland routes, crossing the Sahara – that Europeans first encountered, from the fifteenth century onwards, and that they later tapped into for their initial slave supplies for the Atlantic islands and, later, for the Americas (Map 7).

In the course of their maritime expansion in the fifteenth and sixteenth centuries, Europeans encountered slave systems around the world. The Dutch for example established trading posts in Southeast Asia, where slaves formed

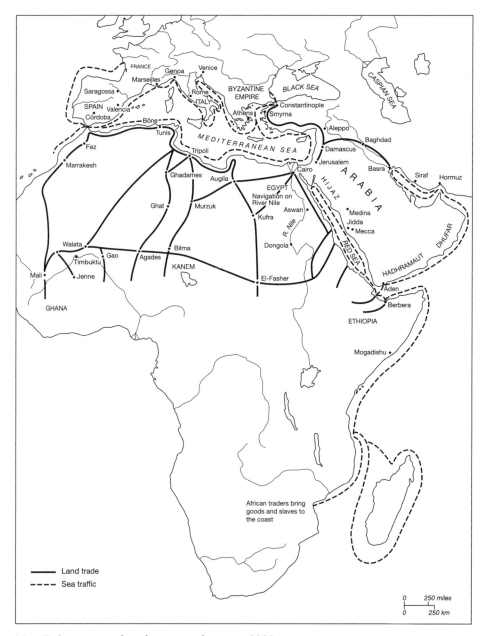

Map 7 Caravan and seaborne trade, c. AD 1000

Source: After Freeman-Grenville, G. S. P. *The New Atlas of African History*, R. G. Collings, p. 47.

a majority of the local urban population (in Malaya, Sumatra and Java). Not surprisingly, the Dutch adapted themselves to local slave systems and, when necessary, imported slaves to serve their own interests. The Dutch also imported slaves from other islands in Southeast Asia and from as far afield as India, Ceylon, Bengal and even Africa. This Dutch demand for slaves in Asia created a widespread and violent slave-trading system and spawned slave-trading states, from Borneo to the Philippines. In their turn, those slave traders' activities ranged as far as the Bay of Bengal. This trade in slaves took on a life of its own, and when Europeans turned against global slavery in the nineteenth century (keen to abolish what they had once sponsored) they found the task daunting and were not able effectively to curb and outlaw slave trading in the region until the late nineteenth century.

Dutch colonial settlements in South Africa were initially founded as way stations for their lucrative trade in Asia. There, and in the Mascarene Islands (Mauritius and Réunion), the Dutch imported slaves mainly from Madagascar and East Africa. Slaves were also moved south to the Cape from other parts of Africa, from Indonesia and from India. India itself had long been home to numbers of slave systems, a fact that the British colonial government simply accepted until the rise of the British abolitionist movement began to target Indian slavery. But before the formal British abolition of slavery in India (in 1843), Indian slaves had been transported to South Africa, the Mascarene Islands, Ceylon and Indonesia (Map 8).

Time and again, then, slavery around the world was sustained by large-scale movements of people; by the enslavement of distant peoples; and by their transportation, by land, water and oceanic crossing, to far-flung slave markets and slave societies. Sometimes the numbers involved were huge. Moreover, most of this was in place *before* the development of the Atlantic slave trade, and much of it survived long *after* slavery in the Americas had been abolished.

The slave systems that developed in the Americas were distinctive, however, not least because they came to be defined by race. Europeans had known about black Africa for centuries before their early maritime contacts with West Africa. Overland trade routes, the overlap of trading and colonial empires in the Mediterranean, the dissemination of myths and rumours (about the peoples and goods of black Africa): all and more had lapped back and forth between Europe and Africa. Trade routes across the Sahara, along the Nile and thence throughout the Mediterranean had brought African and European peoples face to face, although admittedly in very small numbers. Yet there was nothing necessarily *enslaved* about those encounters. Europeans did not assume that the peoples of black Africa were destined to be slaves to white owners or masters. Within a very short space of time, however, Europeans came to view the African as a natural slave, a person to be enslaved and purchased and to be transported in huge numbers over vast distances across the ocean, to work for European settlers on the far side of the Atlantic. Something quite dramatic had changed.

Europeans had effectively dispensed with slavery at home *before* they developed their slave colonies. In the case of England, slavery had died out long ago (though more recently, and less completely, in Scotland). Bondage had been basic to medieval society, and even after the decline of medieval serfdom (itself

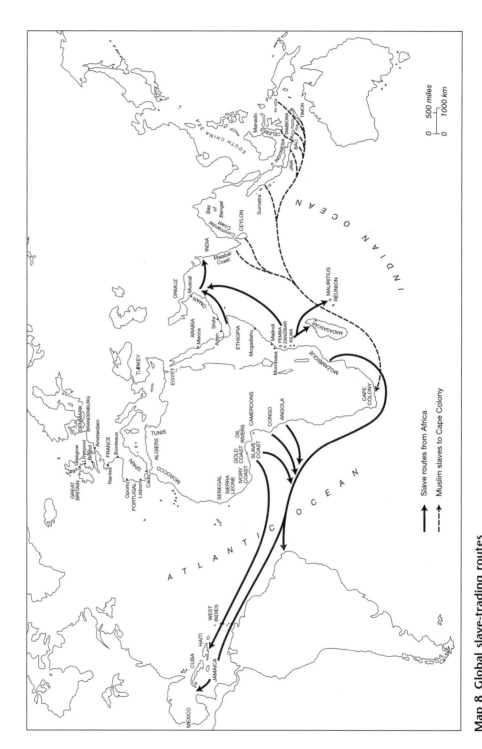

Map 8 Global slave-trading routes
Source: After Freeman-Grenville, G. S. P. *The New Atlas of African History*, R. G. Collings, p. 83.

different from slavery) large numbers of English people were effectively tied to their masters, notably apprentices, pauper children and, until 1772/75, Scottish miners.

But none of these groups were *slaves*, comparable with the Africans shipped into the Americas. Moreover, the forms of slavery that Europeans created in the Americas proved to be among the most hostile and repressive in recorded history. The paradox remains that Europe saw the gradual securing of individual rights to ever more people in Europe *at the very time* that Europeans expanded and intensified slavery across vast tracts of the Americas.

Europeans took small numbers of slaves to the Americas from the early days of exploration. They also enslaved indigenous peoples. The pioneers of that expansion into the Americas were the Spanish and the Portuguese, but from 1580 onwards, the most influential Atlantic migrations fell into the hands of northern Europeans, notably the Dutch and then the English. In the process, and as large parts of the Americas fell under European control, more and more Africans were shipped across the Atlantic. Moreover, substantial proportions of the Europeans who travelled across the Atlantic were also unfree – indentured labourers tied to their masters – but not slaves. Africans began to account for the greater share of all people migrating across the Atlantic, and as slavery developed, the British were critical. Before 1800 nine out of ten people carried into the Americas on British ships were unfree, mainly slaves but also indentured labourers. How did this vast movement of humanity come about? How and why did Europeans turn to Africa for labour and manpower in the Americas?

CHAPTER 2

The ancient world

Slavery was commonplace in a host of ancient and traditional societies. For example, it played a major, integral role in societies from ancient Egypt to the wider world of classical antiquity. Indeed, many of the surviving artifacts and buildings of those societies, now awash with millions of tourists, from the Pyramids to the urban fabric of ancient Greece, were built by slaves. In all those societies, slaves were recruited from outside: by warfare, by raids and kidnapping and by trade and barter in humanity. There were slave markets for the transfer and supply of fresh slaves arriving from the edges of trade and military conquest. Throughout the history of ancient Egypt, large numbers of slaves were acquired by military means (though the slave population also grew of its own accord). The New Kingdom (1560–1070 BC) expanded throughout the present-day Middle East and Sudan; many thousands of Nubians from the Sudan were dragooned as slaves, working in agriculture, in manufacturing and in the military. Females inevitably found their way into domestic slavery. Other African slaves came to Egypt from the coast of Somalia (Map 9).

Greek civilization was equally bound up with slavery, and trade thrived in enslaved peoples, especially in the classical period (450–330 BC). Slaves could be found in large numbers in all the major city-states, where they were bought and sold as objects, with men used in heavy work, women normally in domestic chores. Again, slaves were recruited by violent expeditions. Curiously, the rise of slavery paralleled the rise of Greek democracy, for the slaves gave citizens the freedom to take part in their civic duties. Although slavery changed over time, it became a defining characteristic of Greek civilization. Slaves from the East passed through the Greek slave markets of Chios, Delos and Rhodes (Map 10).

Slavery in the Roman Empire is better known (because more recent and therefore better documented). The successes of the Roman legions throughout that far-flung empire provided legions of slaves for the Roman heartlands, from the northern boundaries of the empire in Britain to the southern limits in Africa. It has been calculated that the golden age of Rome was maintained by the importation of upwards of half a million slaves in one year. Indeed, Roman armies returned in triumph to the imperial capital ahead of their retinue of conquered slaves from as far afield as Germany, Britain and Gaul. Slaves were ubiquitous: as domestics, as labourers in Roman agriculture, in the hell of the mines and, of course, for entertainment in the Colosseum. Few areas of Roman life remained untouched by slaves. Rome may not have been built in a day, but it was certainly built by slaves (Maps 11 and 12).

Slaves in the classical world were acquired through a variety of means: often through the accident of birth (being born to a slave mother) but many came via

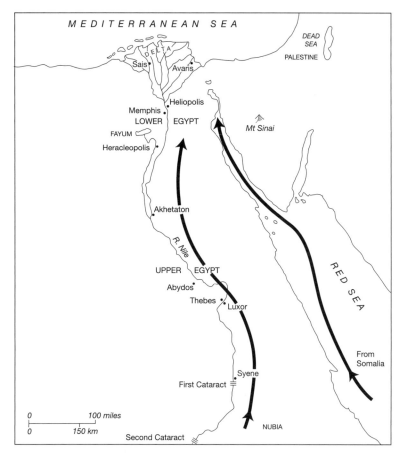

Map 9 Slave routes into ancient Egypt

Source: From *A World History, Third Edition* by William H. McNeill, copyright © 1967, 1971, 1979 by William H. McNeill. Used by permission of Oxford University Press, Inc. and the author.

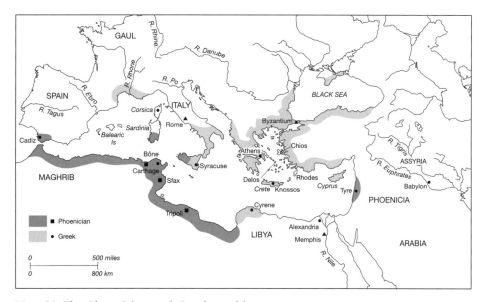

Map 10 The Phoenician and Greek world

Source: After Curtin, P. D. *et al.* (1995) *African History*, Longman, p. 37.

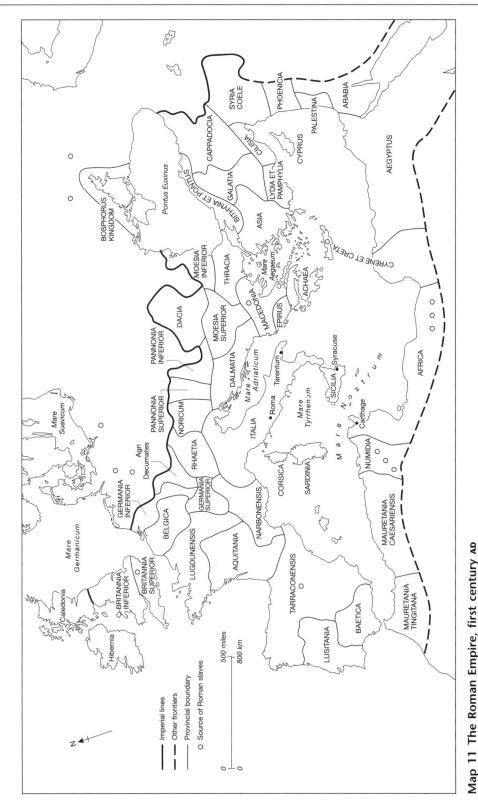

Map 11 The Roman Empire, first century AD

Source: 'Map 8: The Roman Empire, 1st Century AD', from *Europe: A History* by Norman Davies, copyright © 1993 by Norman Davies. Used by permission of Oxford University Press, Inc. and The Random House Group Ltd.

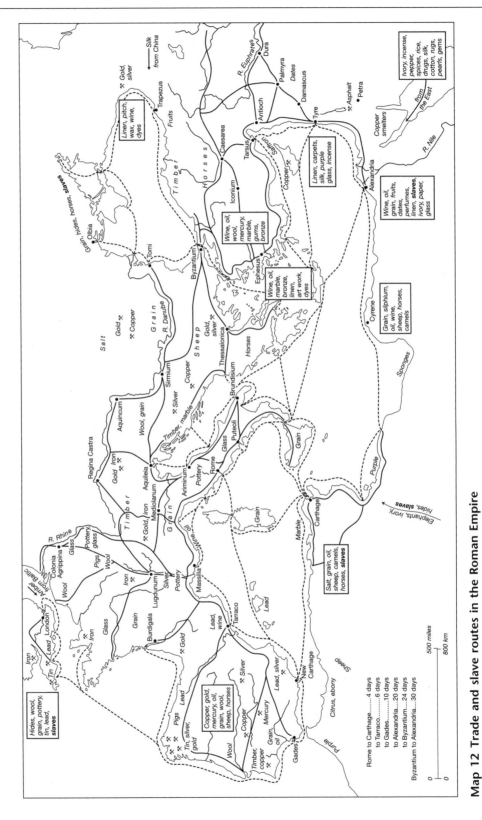

Map 12 Trade and slave routes in the Roman Empire

Source: After Robinson Jr., C. A. (1951) Ancient History: From Prehistoric Times to the Death of Justinian, Macmillan Co., p. 565.

enslavement and transportation over great distances. Greek and Roman civilizations enslaved distant peoples and moved them around the empires, via local slave markets, to be sold and incorporated into the imperial or domestic slave economy. The pattern that emerged later in the Atlantic slave empires (of acquiring and moving slaves great distances) was well established in the classical world (and in Asia). Indeed, the person of the slave often formed a basic article of trade – a commodity – in a large number of pre-modern societies. This was true in Africa, in Celtic Britain and among Indian peoples of North America. Slaves were not the *only* item of trade, of course, but they remained integral to any number of long-distance trading systems in the pre-modern world. But all this assumed that there was a demand for slaves elsewhere: that it was *worth* moving slaves, by land or sea, on long journeys to foreign slave markets.

To modern eyes, slavery in the classical world had curious bedfellows. Chattel slavery (where the slave was a thing) was prominent in Athens at the very time that state became more democratic; perhaps 15–35 percent of the population was enslaved. In Rome, perhaps two million out of a total of six million seems a plausible ratio of slave to free. Greek slaveholders tended to own only small numbers of slaves, but in Rome slaves were often held in large numbers. In fact, even humbler citizens might own a slave. Both Greek and Roman societies chose their slaves from among outsiders ('barbarians') though, unlike slavery later in the Americas, it was not defined in racial terms. Warfare and kidnapping provided the main source of slaves, and the massive expansion of the Roman Empire and the successes of the Roman legions yielded huge numbers of slaves for the imperial heartlands.

Specialist slave traders were common in the Mediterranean (though they often traded in other commodities as well as humans). These human commodities eventually found their way to the major slave markets in urban areas. Not surprisingly, slaves in the classical world were to be found in all corners of the classical economy, in agriculture, in mining, in domestic service and even in skilled occupations. Slaves were used for any numbers of functions. They undertook the most back-breaking work in construction, mining and agriculture. They toiled in the galleys. But they could also be found in a range of skilled occupations and in trusted household positions. The richer the slave owners, the larger the number of slaves likely to work in their homes. In Rome, there were enslaved firemen, secretaries and doctors.

Given the extent of the civilizations of Egypt, Greece and Rome, Africans could be found among the exotic people of the imperial heartlands. Africans from Ethiopia were dispersed throughout the Mediterranean and naturally enough appear on a range of contemporary artifacts, from pottery to paintings. Similarly, surviving scraps of contemporary writing also capture the African presence in the world of classical antiquity. But the blackness of Africans did *not* denote slavery. Slaves in antiquity were more likely to be white than black, and there is no evidence that Greece and Rome regarded blacks as their natural inferiors (Map 13).

Because classical civilization was so dependent on slaves, there was a great deal of political and philosophical debate about slavery and about the legality and status of slaves in both Greek and Roman texts. Greek law, Greek writers,

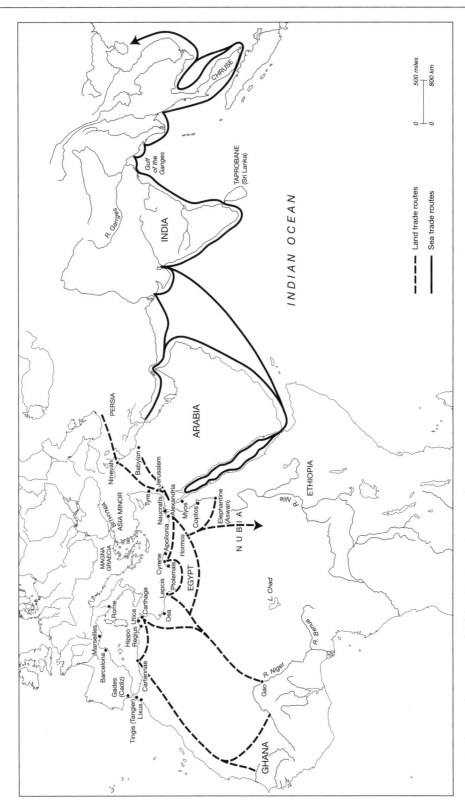

Map 13 The trade routes of Africa in Greco-Roman times
Source: After Freeman-Grenville, G. S. P. *The New Atlas of African History*, R. G. Collings, p. 25.

playwrights and philosophers all discussed the role of slavery. Though there were disagreements about the rationale for slavery, few doubted the importance and existence of slavery. In classical Rome, where the law established a distinction between a slave and a serf, criticism of slavery tended to concentrate on the *abuses* of the local slave system, rather than on the institution itself. In time, legal changes were introduced to restrict the maltreatment of slaves, though without infringing the principle that the master should own the slave much like any other piece of property. The coming of Christianity tended to moderate the worst abuses of Roman slavery, but it did not, initially at least, undermine slavery itself. Everywhere, the slave systems of classical antiquity attracted little criticism: slavery was too embedded in the social system to be criticized, still less dispensed with. Nor did early Christianity pose any real threat to slavery. It continued to be viable and was generally unchallenged.

CHAPTER 3

Overland African slave routes

Europe first effectively encountered Africans courtesy of the overland trading routes from black Africa. Africans had long been familiar in Mediterranean societies. As we have seen, large number of Africans had been transported to ancient Egypt. And the Roman Empire, along the southern rim of the Mediterranean, had also incorporated Africans via the trading routes down the Nile and overland across the desert to West and Central Africa. Indeed, African labour remained in demand in the Mediterranean long after the collapse of Rome.

The spread of Islam from the eighth century onwards accentuated the demand for black slaves, and Islamic overland trade routes ensured regular supplies right through to the modern era (Map 14). Black African slaves were employed in all North African countries, from Egypt in the east to Morocco on the Atlantic coast. Some of those Africans inevitably found their way to northern Europe.

There were four main slave trade routes crossing the Sahara to Morocco, Tunisia and Libya: from Timbuktu, Kano, Bornu (Lake Chad) and Wadai. But each of these locations had complementary and overlapping trade routes to the south, deeper into Africa (Map 15). It was a system that lasted for more than a millennium (compared with the 400 years of the Atlantic slave trade). Inevitably, the figures involved are elusive, and estimates of the total number of Africans crossing the Sahara as slaves vary, ranging from three and a half million to almost seven million. However, no one doubts that the source of those slaves was generally violent capture.

African slaves were brought overland along with other more traditional forms of trade. Egypt was an established centre for the trade in African slaves, and though the early evidence is sparse, it is clear enough that many thousands of Africans passed through the slave markets of Cairo *en route* to other Mediterranean destinations. In addition, large numbers remained in Egypt to work as slaves. Again, Islam accentuated the process of slave trading in and through Egypt. This was a slaving system that was only effectively ended within living memory. The majority of Africans transported in this way were women, destined for domestic service and concubinage. When large numbers of Africans began to be shipped across the Atlantic, the majority of its victims were men: the parallel slave trade north, within Africa, was a trade in women.

The consequences of these enslaved African migrations northwards was that Africans formed noticeable groups throughout the urban settlements of the greater Mediterranean region, from Cairo to Istanbul, transplanting into those

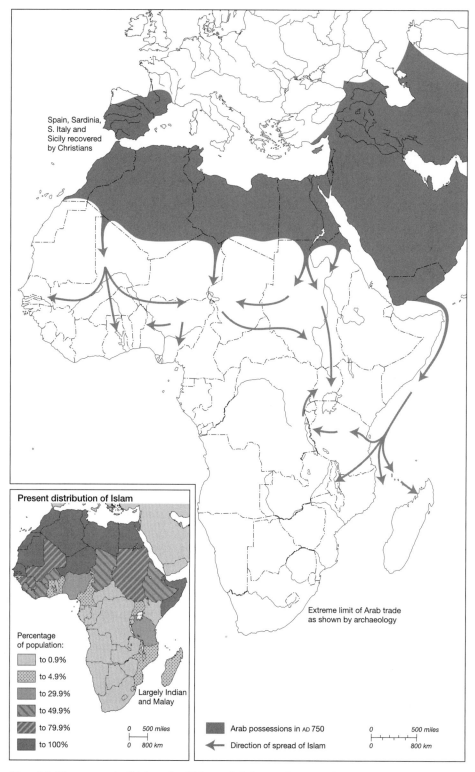

Spain, Sardinia, S. Italy and Sicily recovered by Christians

Present distribution of Islam

Percentage of population:

to 0.9%

to 4.9%

to 29.9%

to 49.9%

to 79.9%

to 100%

Largely Indian and Malay

0   500 miles
0   800 km

Extreme limit of Arab trade as shown by archaeology

Arab possessions in AD 750

Direction of spread of Islam

0   500 miles
0   800 km

Map 14 The spread of Islam in Africa, eighth to nineteenth century
Source: After Freeman-Grenville, G. S. P. *The New Atlas of African History*, R. G. Collings, p. 43.

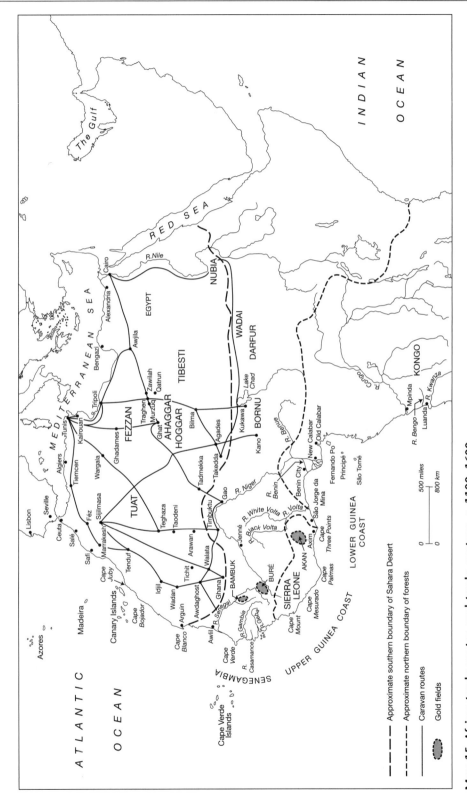

Map 15 Africa: trade routes and trade centres, c. 1100–1600

Source: After Phillips, W. D. (1985) *Slavery from Roman Times to the Early Atlantic Slave Trade*, University of Minnesota Press, p. 115.

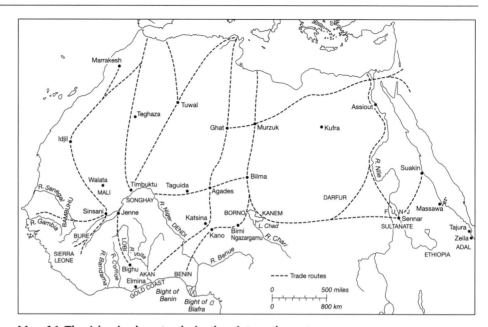

Map 16 The Islamic slave trade in the sixteenth century
Source: After Lovejoy, P. E. (1983) *Transformations in Slavery: A History of Slavery in Africa*,
Cambridge University Press, p. 26.

communities a variety of African cultural habits (notably religions).[1] Much the
same was to happen in the Americas.

The figures for the trans-Saharan trade suggest that, over a long span, the
numbers of slaves transported overland from Africa amounted to more than half
the numbers shipped into the Americas. Recent evidence suggests that slavery
and slave trading in this region have not been totally eradicated even at the
time of writing (Map 16).

---

[1] Ralph Austen, 'The Mediterranean Islamic slave trade out of Africa: a tentative census',
in Patrick Manning (ed.), *Slave Trades, 1500–1800*, Aldershot, 1996, Ch.1.

CHAPTER 4

European slavery and slave trades

Between the fall of Rome and the decline of feudalism – a period of some 1,000 years – slavery and other forms of bondage were as common in Europe as in other continents. Those European slave systems often depended as much on imported supplies of slaves from other parts of the world as they did on whatever natural increase took place in the slave populations. Both in the Byzantine Empire to the east and in Western Europe, slavery was not only commonplace; it was also essential to the way local societies functioned. In the West, however, slavery was to fade away and die.

The evidence that describes the nature and complexities of slavery and slave trading in early medieval Europe is fragmentary and sparse, but the broad pattern seems clear enough. In Western Europe, the emergence of feudalism saw the rise of a system that depended for its agricultural labour force on unfree serfs and slaves. It was a system often supported by draconian slave codes that relegated the slave to a position nearer to the animal kingdom than to humanity. In England, the widespread use of slaves was reflected in the *Domesday Book* of 1086, though by then it was clearly in decline. But in the course of that century it is generally true that slavery was giving way to the rise of a free peasantry.

International slave trading was also widespread, with slaves recruited from the very edges of Europe, from the Balkans (hence slavs = slaves), though sometimes they came from even further afield. Sporadic slave raids and trading covered huge tracts of land and ocean, with the Vikings (notably against the Irish) and the Magyars weaving a violent slave-trading web that stretched from Iceland to Central Asia. Slaves were shifted back and forth, into Europe and from Europe, along well-defined slave routes, to and from the slave markets of the Mediterranean and Arab societies (see Map 3). Overall, the centres of slavery and slave trading in early medieval Europe seem to have been the major ports and cities. Though the institution of slavery was in decline in Western Europe between 500 and 1,000, it was really in the later Middle Ages that rural slavery declined markedly. Thereafter, European slavery was primarily domestic (and therefore female), with slaves from the eastern Mediterranean imported through major ports in Italy and Spain. From the twelfth to the fifteenth century, Western European rural life came to be dominated not by slavery but by serfdom and a free peasantry.

Until the mid-twelfth century, European slavery was maintained by importing slaves. Equally, European slaves were transported to distant slave societies. Vikings, for example, attacked and captured people around their periphery, shifting people from Ireland to Iceland. Scandinavian slave traders took people from Britain, selling them on to distant slave markets, sometimes as far away as the Mediterranean. Viking slave routes took captives as far afield as Greenland and, by river and overland routes, to the Middle East and Central Asia. It was, overall, a blurred network of violent trading and enslavement that saw valued commodities traded and retraded for other goods, with slaves captured *en route*, before contact was made with Muslim traders to the east. However, most slaves captured by the predatory Vikings were not sold on but were used by the Vikings themselves in settling a region that they had plundered and then claimed as their own. It is hard to be precise about the numbers of slaves involved, but it has been suggested that, around 950, perhaps 15 percent of Europe's population of some 22+ million was enslaved. At the time of the Norman Conquest, the enslaved population of England ranged between 10 and 20 percent. For all this, however, it is clear enough that slavery became less important in late medieval Europe than in earlier epochs (Map 17).

Slavery in medieval Europe was greatly affected by the rapid rise of Islam, which, from the eighth century onwards, spread into Europe, across the Middle East and North Africa, and deep into black Africa. Like Christianity, Islam was committed to the belief that it was wrong to enslave co-religionists, but Islamic expansion and military successes enabled huge numbers of alien (including Christian) captives and prisoners of war to be enslaved. New Islamic states everywhere incorporated foreign slaves and relied on traders to bring slaves in, most strikingly perhaps in the form of female slavery and concubinage. In the process, Christian Europe found itself pitted against an expansionist Islam, and both sides enslaved the other (during the Crusades for example). Muslim power was finally removed from Spain only in 1492 – the year of Columbus's first voyage to the west. The two events were linked, because one impulse behind European maritime exploration was the determination to outflank the world of Islam.

On the eve of their maritime adventures in the Atlantic (first to Africa, later to the Americas), European powers had long been familiar with African slavery and slave routes. Although indigenous slavery had died out in Western Europe, the enslavement of others (more especially Muslims, and of Christians by Muslims) was common. Indeed, the persistent (and at times wholesale) capture of Christian sailors and travellers by Islamic powers in North Africa remained a persistent problem into the eighteenth century.

However, there was another (and in the long term perhaps more important) link between medieval slavery and the Americas. Crusaders had brought back sugar cane from the eastern Mediterranean, and sugar cane cultivation – on plantations – spread, first to southern Europe, later into the Atlantic islands. This taste for sugar and for sweetness in food and drink was first conceived in the Mediterranean, where the development of the local sugar industry was closely linked to slavery in the region. At a time when slavery had effectively vanished in northern Europe and had died out in other forms of Mediterranean agriculture, slaves were introduced into sugar cultivation. It is true that small-scale slavery survived in other areas of the Mediterranean on the galleys, in harems and in domestic service – but it was now, in addition, linked to sugar plantations. By the end of the sixteenth century, however, the European sweet tooth was to be

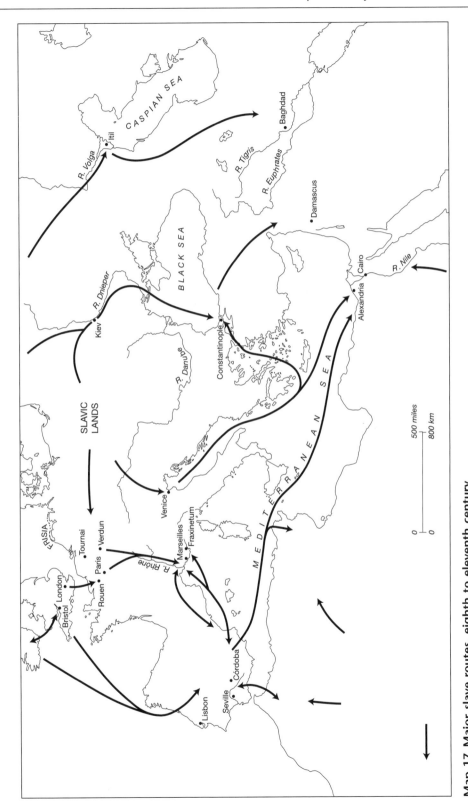

Map 17 Major slave routes, eighth to eleventh century
Source: After Phillips, W. D. (1985) *Slavery from Roman Times to the Early Atlantic Slave Trade*, University of Minnesota Press, p. 44.

satisfied by very different plantation workers: Africans toiling on the plantations of the Americas. Yet a curious fact remains. With these exceptions in the Mediterranean, Europeans had effectively abandoned slavery at home *at the very moment* that they began to turn to slavery in their new-found lands in the Atlantic and in the Americas.

CHAPTER 5

Exploration and the spread of sugar

The 'age of exploration' of the fifteenth and sixteenth centuries took Europeans to the Americas, to West Africa and to Asia and was prompted by a host of factors: by simple curiosity, by the urge to trade, and by the Christian zeal to outflank Islam. The prime movers were the Spaniards and Portuguese in the fifteenth century, though the urge to explore had roots further back in European experience. Italians and other European trading peoples had long been interested in expanding their horizons by breaking out of the restrictions of traditional European trading routes, notably in the Mediterranean. Though some had reached the Canaries, Madeira and the Azores, the limitations of contemporary navigation, ship construction and cartography (to say nothing of the fear of the unknown) all conspired to limit trade and navigation primarily to the Mediterranean and to coastal waters. But in a number of European trading ports and cities, merchants and learned men had begun to accumulate information about the attractions of Africa, especially its gold, its spices and its slaves. The Portuguese in particular were drawn to the idea of maritime trade to Africa, especially after their conquest of the North African city of Ceuta in 1415. Portuguese determination to tap into the wealth and potential of Africa by sea increased: to go direct to the source of goods and prosperity that had previously reached Europe by overland routes.

What Portugal's monarch, Prince Henry the Navigator, wanted was direct maritime access to the gold that came from Guinea. Gathering a group of experienced and learned men to the cause, Henry improved the Portuguese port of Lagos and constructed the most up-to-date vessels for the enterprise of exploring the African coastline. Moving in stages, the Portuguese took and settled *en route* Madeira (*c.* 1420) and the Azores (1427), later the Cape Verde Islands (1456–60). There they introduced sugar planting. As the Portuguese edged further south along the African coast, successive voyages returned to Portugal with more and more detailed information for subsequent voyages. In 1442, one ship returned with gold, salt and a group of Africans. Each subsequent Portuguese voyage travelling ever further south returned with African goods, acquired initially from Muslim traders. A number of them had African slaves, most of whom had been captured in war or in raids. It became clear that it was easier (more practical and simpler) to buy Africans rather than try to snatch them. By 1448, the Portuguese had shipped perhaps 1,000 Africans back to Portugal, or to their Atlantic islands. Yet African slaves had not been the *reason* for Portuguese travels to Africa; nor were they the main source of trade.

By the 1460s they were trading in Sierra Leone, and twenty years later they had entered the Congo. By then, they wanted not only African goods but also a route south and east – to Asia. By 1488, Bartholomeu Diaz had rounded the Cape of Good Hope: 'for the promise it gave of finding India'. A decade later, Vasco da Gama had sailed around the Cape, then north along the East African coast and into the complex systems of existing Islamic trading and sailing routes across the Indian Ocean. European traders had thus found the oceanic way open to India, and thence to China and Southeast Asia (Map 18).

In West Africa, the Portuguese were attracted to two specific regions for gold: first to the Gambia, with its access to the interior gold fields, and second to the Gold Coast, where, in 1480, they began to build their forts, the first at Elmina, to protect their gold. In time, all the major European trading rivals constructed forts along that coast, initially to guard their gold, later their slaves. With a permanent position on the coast, the Portuguese were now able to trade in slaves *between* different African societies. At first, the volume of this slave trade was small and was a minor activity set against trade in other African commodities. However, all this changed courtesy of events on the other side of the Atlantic. What transformed the history of African slavery was the story of sugar.

Sugar cane cultivation had moved gradually westwards from various spots in the Middle East and the southern Mediterranean (its indigenous home had been in Southeast Asia) (Map 19). Throughout the late Middle Ages cane sugar had been exotic and therefore costly in Europe, but as European explorers and settlers, led by the Portuguese, moved out of the Mediterranean they discovered new opportunities for cultivating crops in their new settlements. Thus sugar was transported by both the Spanish and the Portuguese to Madeira and the Canaries, later to the islands in the Gulf of Guinea (São Tomé, Fernando Po and Principé). The Portuguese and Spanish experimented with various forms of trans-planted agriculture, adopting where appropriate the plantation system already long in use in the Mediterranean. The technology, finance and skills of sugar cultivation long perfected in the Mediterranean were now transferred to the Atlantic islands and the sugar shipped direct to northern Europe. When sugar was cultivated in São Tomé – close to the African coast – African slaves were used as labourers. All this prompted a growing European demand for cane sugar, though still on a small scale, and the amount of sugar remained limited. Then, in the early sixteenth century, sugar was transplanted to new settlements in the Americas (Map 20).

Columbus (familiar with the sugar business in Madeira) carried sugar cane (and other crops) on his second voyage in 1493. Ten years later, sugar was introduced to Santo Domingo (using men trained in sugar cultivation from the Canary Islands) and by 1570 about 1,000 tons was being produced there each year. Sugar production spread to neighbouring Spanish West Indian islands, notably Jamaica and Puerto Rico. But Spanish interest in the Caribbean islands was restricted by their greater interest in the wealth and potential elsewhere: in Mexico and elsewhere in Central America. The islands were useful way stations to and from the apparent abundance of Central and South America. As a result, Spanish sugar production in the islands remained small, and the potential limited, until the English settled their own West Indian islands in the early seventeenth century.

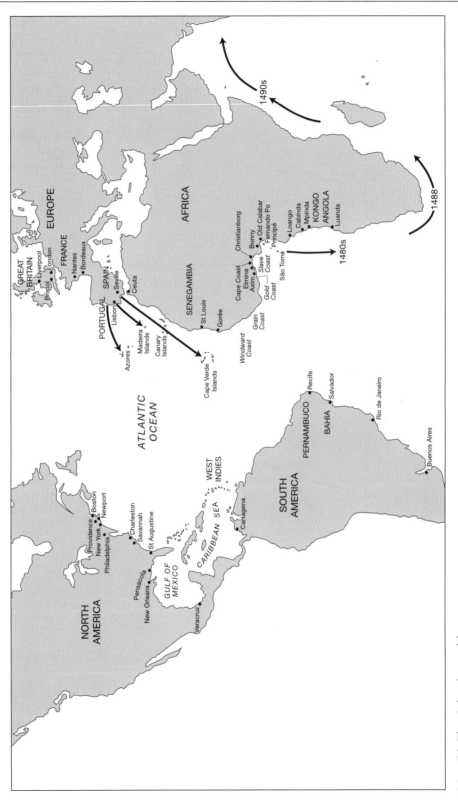

Map 18 The Atlantic world

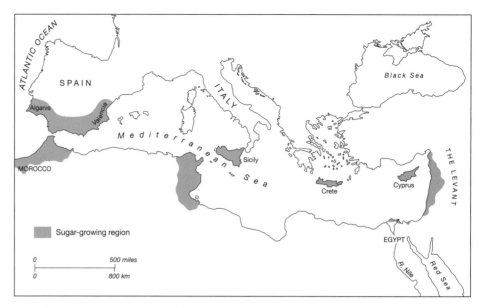

Map 19 Sugar cultivation in the Mediterranean
Source: After Curtin, P. D. (1990) *The Rise and Fall of the Plantation Complex: Essays in Atlantic History, 1st Edition*, Cambridge University Press, p. 19.

Map 20 The westward migration of sugar planting
Source: After Curtin, P. D. *et al.* (1995) *African History*, Longman, p. 217.

The take-off of sugar took place not in the Caribbean but in Brazil, where sugar had been transplanted from Madeira in the 1540s. Within twenty years, 2,500 tons of Brazilian sugar was being produced each year. By 1600, that figure had grown to 16,000 tons, and thirty years later it stood at 20,000 tons. Brazil now produced ten times as much sugar as any other colony in the Americas.

This dramatic growth in Brazilian sugar production was made possible by ideal environmental factors and by a growing reliance on imported African labour. European settlers had introduced exotic crops into the Americas, using European finance to fund their experiments, and they relied on the technical expertise acquired in sugar production on the Atlantic islands. However, the essential manpower came increasingly from Africa. Moreover, it was enslaved – not free – labour. As the Brazilian sugar industry expanded and thrived in the late sixteenth century, it did so on the backs of armies of imported African slaves.

CHAPTER 6

Europeans, slaves and West Africa

The Portuguese led the way in the maritime exploration and development of the initial commercial links with West Africa, and they were able to do so through the complexity of political and maritime advantages they enjoyed. Portuguese sailors returned home from the early voyages with Africans (enslaved and free), and small numbers of Africans were soon to be found scattered across Portugal (Map 21).

Returning vessels, discharging their cargoes at Portuguese quaysides, revealed Africa's riches and potential, inevitably attracting the envious attention of other European commercial and maritime interests. European maritime states and commercial groups could not resist the temptation to follow the Portuguese lead to tap into the prosperity of the wider world. In common with the Portuguese, they were attracted initially *not* by Africans but rather by the other appealing goods and commodities that Africa had to offer.

On the African coast, the early European traders encountered a series of African trading systems (trades in nuts, foodstuffs, textiles, gold – and slaves), which reached from the coast into the interior. However, disease made West Africa a dangerous place for Europeans to trade, and to settle. From the first, Europeans learned that it was prudent to sail away as soon as trade and weather allowed. Lingering on the coast inevitably brought sickness and rising death rates among the European crews.

Though Europeans bought and shipped African slaves from their first encounters on the coast, at first slaves were of minor interest. In the words of Philip Curtin, slaves were 'a fortuitous and unexpected by-product of the gold trade' (Map 22).

The prime attraction was gold, acquired along the Gambia River from interior gold fields, and on the Gold Coast with its access to the Akan gold fields. In both places, and in Benin and Congo, slaves were also available and the Portuguese began to dabble in African slavery, buying, selling and transporting Africans from one part of the coast to another. They also used the island of São Tomé both as an *entrepôt* and for sugar cultivation – again using African slaves. The numbers of slaves involved were small, but all that changed from about 1550 onwards, when upheaval in Congo made available growing numbers of slaves on the coast and when sugar cultivation took root on the far side of the Atlantic in Brazil.

Even so, until about 1600, demand in the Americas for African slaves remained relatively small. Indeed, more slaves continued to be moved across the Sahara than across the Atlantic. Thereafter, the massive expansion of the Atlantic slave trade was to redirect this flow of African peoples. In the process,

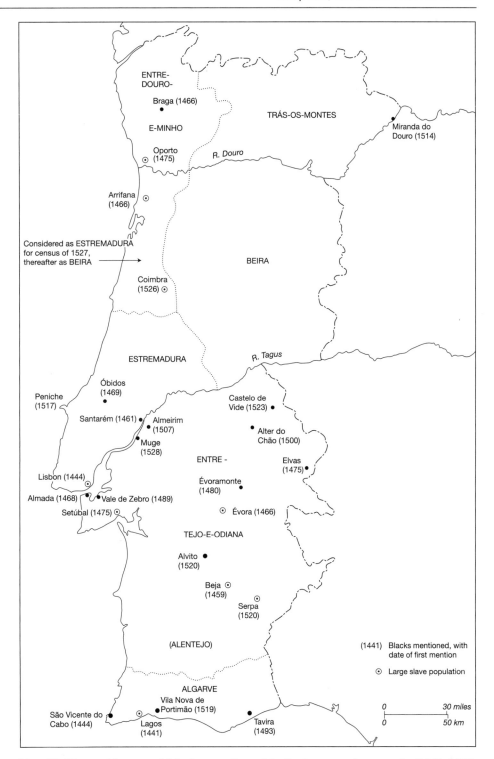

Map 21 The residences of blacks mentioned in Portuguese documents, 1441–1530
Source: After Saunders, A. (1982) *A Social History of Black Slaves and Freedmen in Portugal,*
1441–1555, Cambridge University Press, p. 51.

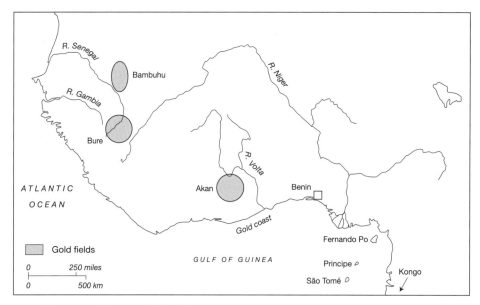

Map 22 West African gold fields
Source: After Curtin, P. D. (1990) *The Rise and Fall of the Plantation Complex: Essays in Atlantic History, 1st Edition*, Cambridge University Press, p. 44.

the Atlantic slave trade generated a whole new industry, of African and European traders and middlemen, who henceforth dispatched their captives not towards the traditional overland northern routes but westwards, towards the European traders on the Atlantic coast, thence on to the slave ships bound for the Americas. The overland African routes continued, but their numbers were soon dwarfed by the legions of Africans loaded on to the slave ships.

Ever more European traders found themselves drawn irresistibly to the African coast. Until the mid-sixteenth century, Portuguese merchants carried most of the slaves from Africa, their slave ship captains conducting business from on board their vessels, anchored on the African coast or in river estuaries. Many of those slaves went to the Atlantic islands and to Europe itself, in total, before 1500, fewer perhaps than 2,000 a year. But numbers gradually increased. By the late 1520s, perhaps 2,000 were being shipped into São Tomé each year. From the 1550s, however, Brazilian sugar plantations wanted their own supplies of Africans.

By then, other Europeans had staked their claim to trade in African humanity. From the mid-sixteenth century, Spanish merchants (notably from Seville) began their own slaving voyages to West Africa, often with financial support from Italian merchants and backers. From its earliest days, the slave trade thus attracted merchant capitalism from throughout Europe's scattered commercial and financial communities. Few felt that their money and investments were following an immoral or unethical route. There was money to be made in West Africa, and especially in shipping labour from the African coast to new European settlements in the Americas. If traders felt moral qualms about this drift into the slave trade, they rarely said so. Europeans were united (if by nothing else) by the increasingly powerful attraction to invest in African humanity.

The early years of European trading on the African coast were small-scale and piecemeal, and most of the first African slaves were shipped to Europe or to the Atlantic islands. From 1518 onwards, however, with the granting of the Spanish *asientos*, which were licences to take Africans into the Spanish Americas, the Atlantic slave trade came into its own, developing a structure and nature that was to characterize the trade for centuries. For their part, the Spanish were never to become major traders on the African coast, preferring instead to settle their American colonies with African slaves bought from other slave traders. In the event, a total of almost 1.7 million Africans were shipped into Spanish America.

What drove forward the Atlantic slave trade was the creation of the sugar plantations, first in Brazil, later in the West Indies. It also required the ability and willingness of ever more Europeans to enter the African and the Atlantic slave system and to establish their slave-based economies in the Americas. In the process, three continents became locked together, but the human lubricant of the whole system was the African slave. To secure those slaves in the numbers required, and at affordable prices, all Europeans needed to secure their own *entrée* to the politics and trade of West Africa.

As the slave trade increased (dramatically after 1600), ever more Europeans sought a toehold on the coast as the best way of guaranteeing their own share of the lucrative trade across the Atlantic. Thus the initial Portuguese monopoly on the coast was challenged, particularly when sugar cultivation spread from Brazil to the Caribbean in the early seventeenth century. At the same time, newly emergent European powers began to flex their own commercial and maritime muscles, seeking a profitable share both in the trade to and from Africa and in the settlement of the Americas. The Dutch led the way, driven forward by the remarkable maritime and commercial strength that shaped the 'Dutch Golden Age'. Though a nation of a mere 1.5 million people, the Dutch became a global maritime power, greatly helped by their perfection of the joint stock system. Amsterdam and Rotterdam became the financial and commercial heart of that Dutch commercial empire, attracting money and expertise from elsewhere in Europe. That money and commercial know-how were directed to the economic potential in the Atlantic (and in Asia). As the power of the Dutch, later the English, rose in the seventeenth century, the power of Spain and Portugal declined.

The Dutch had shown some initial reluctance to accept African slaves in Holland itself, but such moral scruples were unusual among Europeans, who had by, say, 1600 come to terms with the African as an item of international trade. Moral sensitivity was quickly relegated to the commercial benefits of shipping Africans into the Americas. The first Atlantic slaving voyages were *ad hoc* and small-scale, sometimes involving capturing Africans from other European slave traders, but the key to long-term success in this trade was having a viable, manageable base on the African coast itself. Again, it was a pattern dictated by events in the Americas. Once the Dutch had briefly taken northern Brazil from the Portuguese in 1630, they had the incentive to secure their own bases in Africa for the supply of slaves. By then, some 400,000 Africans had already been shipped by the Portuguese. As Portugal weakened and its imperial power waned, the Dutch stepped in, taking chunks of the former Portuguese empire in Africa, Asia and the Americas. After numerous small-scale visits, the

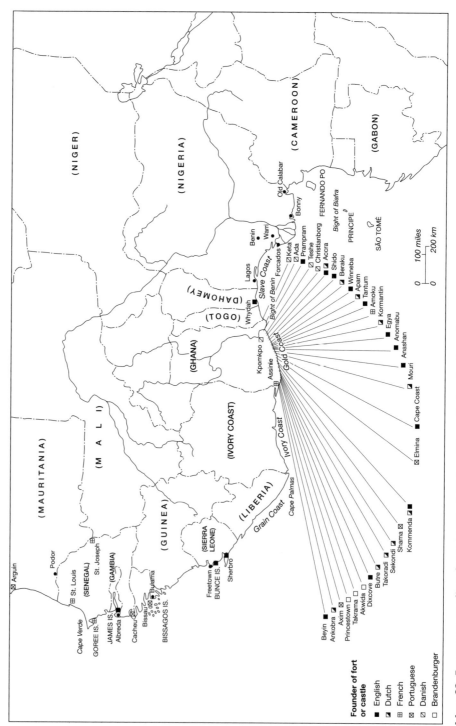

Map 23 European trading forts in West Africa, fifteenth to nineteenth century
Source: After Freeman-Grenville, G. S. P. *The New Atlas of African History*, R. G. Collings, Map 51.

Dutch established their first base on the African coast in 1612 (at Mouri, in present-day Ghana). Within a decade, the Dutch had become *the* main traders on the Gold Coast, later taking over the Portuguese post at Elmina and finally removing them from São Tomé, Annabon, São Paula, Benguela and then Axim. By the 1640s, the Dutch were the main European presence on the African coast. Inevitably, other European maritime powers were anxious to put down their own trading roots on the African coast, prompted by the success of their own early voyages, which had been mainly privateering, but in this next phase of Atlantic slavery, the British were to prove the key players (Map 23).

CHAPTER 7

Britain, slavery and the slave trade

Before the British entered the Atlantic slave trade, some 630,000 Africans had already been shipped across the Atlantic, but like others before them, English sailors and merchants were attracted to the commercial temptations of West Africa and other distant destinations. There had been a growing English interest in oceanic trade and adventure from the late fifteenth century onwards, notably from Bristol, prompted in part by the Venetian John Cabot's interest in the Atlantic. A number of efforts were made to open sea links across the North Atlantic, but the region to the south looked more promising, not least because contacts with Iberian sailors and traders confirmed the benefits to be had from the routes already pioneered by the Spanish and Portuguese. Drake's circumnavigation of the world (1577–1580), followed by Thomas Cavendish (1586–1588), confirmed the prospects (and dangers) of oceanic trade and adventure. Settlement and trade began to beckon in all corners of the globe in the late sixteenth century. Efforts to settle North America, for example, were paralleled by trading ventures to the East, to the Mediterranean and to Africa, mainly by chartered trading companies in the late years of the sixteenth century.

Mercantile links with Spanish and Portuguese traders dealing directly with West Africa confirmed Africa's commercial potential. From the 1550s onwards, merchants in the West Country and London financed a number of English voyages (notably Thomas Wyndham's) to West Africa (in search of spices, ivory and gold – though some returned with slaves). These English voyages inevitably intruded into what the Portuguese regarded as their own sphere of trade and interest. Then, in 1562, John Hawkins made what was effectively the first English slave-trading voyage. Hawkins was already familiar with the Canaries (where Africans worked as slaves), and now he took three vessels, first to Tenerife, thence to Sierra Leone, where he 'got into his possession, partly by the sworde, and partly by other meanes, to the number of 3,000 Negros at the least'. Hawkins sailed to the Spanish West Indian island of Hispaniola, where he sold all his slaves 'with prosperous success and much gaine to himselfe and the aforesayde adventurers [his backers]'. But such ventures were few and spasmodic until the early seventeenth century, when new British trading companies began to open up the African trade (Map 24).

However, more immediately attractive than Africa were the pickings to be had from the vulnerable Spanish empire in the Caribbean and Central America. The Spanish had tried to license and control the flow of Africans into their possessions, and Hawkins' three slave-trading voyages of 1562–1568 had broken into that Spanish monopoly, compounding Spanish grievances against the English. In addition, the Caribbean initially offered treasure far beyond the

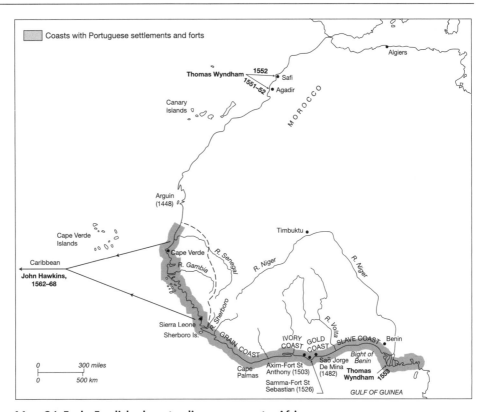

Map 24 Early English slave-trading voyages to Africa
Source: After Porter, A. (ed.) (1991) *Atlas of British Overseas Expansion*, Routledge, p. 19.

profits of slave trading. West Country privateers – most notably Drake – preyed on Spanish settlements and on the treasure fleets passing through the Caribbean on the way home to Spain. In the years 1586–1603, for example, an estimated 235 such privateers plied their trade around the Caribbean. Such voyages inflicted great damage on Spain, but they also helped to develop the English fleet and provided important experience of long-distance oceanic trade and warfare. They also helped to lay the foundations for British settlement in the Caribbean in the early seventeenth century. By the 1620s, the British had recognized the attractions of trade and settlement in the Caribbean and had begun the settlement of their own islands in St Kitts (1624) and Barbados (1625) (Map 25).

The emergence of a British presence and power in the region was aided by the erosion of both Spain and Portugal, weakened by upheavals at home and by the military and commercial attacks of the Dutch abroad. In addition, the disasters of the Thirty Years War (1618–1648) wrought havoc in mainland Europe, distracting the main adversaries from overseas matters. Britain, relatively untouched by those upheavals (until its own civil war in 1642), had groups of enterprising investors and merchants (including influential men in and around the royal court) who were alert to global commercial opportunities and were keen to take advantage of their rivals' problems. Thus did the British (now not merely the English) begin to develop an interest in the slave trade.

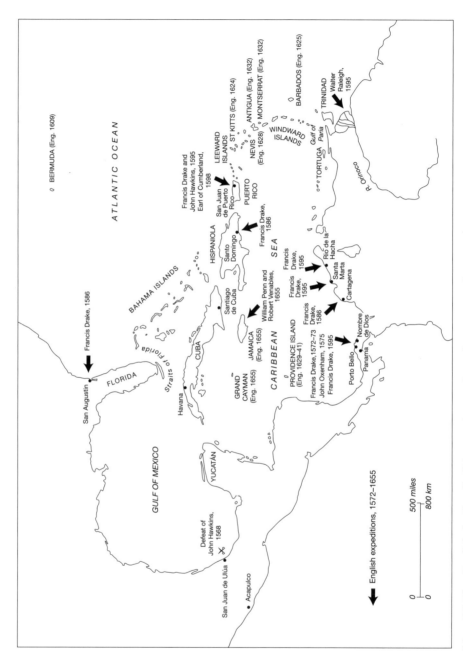

Map 25 The English in the Caribbean, sixteenth and seventeenth centuries
Source: After Porter, A. (ed.) (1991) *Atlas of British Overseas Expansion*, Routledge, p. 25.

The transformation of the British slave trade from the *ad hoc* raids of Hawkins and others into a vast, well-organized industry was made possible by events in the Americas. As with Spain and Portugal in the sixteenth century, the British slave trade in the seventeenth century grew in response to the creation of a new sugar industry – this time in the Caribbean, especially in Barbados. After experimenting with various export crops, the newly founded West Indian colonies turned to sugar cultivation. They also turned to African slaves to work on the plantations. The expansion of sugar paralleled the rise of slavery across the British Caribbean. In 1651, Barbados exported 3,750 tons of sugar to England, expanding to 9,525 tons by 1669. In that same period, the slave population grew from about 20,000 to about 30,000. By then, the island's black population greatly outnumbered the white.

Barbados became the pacemaker both for sugar production (helping to create the infamous British sweet tooth) and for imports of Africans. After 1655, however, that role was usurped by Jamaica (seized by Cromwell from the Spanish in that year). By 1700, Jamaica's black population had climbed to 42,000, compared with 7,300 whites. Almost fifty years later it stood at 118,000, as opposed to 10,400 whites. The rise of sugar production throughout the British Caribbean involved the importation of ever more African slaves: as the British became the dominant colonizers in the West Indies, they also became the dominant slave traders in the Atlantic.

A similar process unfolded in Britain's Chesapeake colonies of Virginia and Maryland. There, the development of late seventeenth-century tobacco plantations saw the importing of increasing numbers of Africans, though never on the scale or intensity to be found in the sugar islands. The conversion of South Carolina to rice cultivation (again on plantations) in the 1690s was also made possible by imported Africans. Thus, in the late seventeenth century, the British became *the* major Atlantic slave traders: between 1660 and 1700, they shipped almost a third of a million Africans across the Atlantic. The small handful of slaving privateers of the late sixteenth century had grown to hundreds of vessels by the late seventeenth century; by the late eighteenth century, thousands of slave ships were involved. By 1700, say, when the British had secured their colonies in North America and the Caribbean, the labour demands of many (though not all) of those colonies were largely satisfied by armies of African slaves. In the process, the British had created a major new industry: their own Atlantic slave trade.

To satisfy the voracious demand for Africans in British American colonies, new ways of trading were devised. The early trade and sugar industry had relied on Dutch finance and experience (of sugar cultivation in Brazil), but that soon gave way to a British insistence on their own monopoly of supplying slaves to their own colonies (a pattern common to most European slave-trading nations in their early stages). The Royal African Company (though it had earlier monopolistic forebears) was founded in 1672 and granted the monopoly to ship Africans to the British American colonies. All sorts and conditions of Britons invested in the company: royalty, the Court and the City. As the slave-based economies flourished in British America, the Royal African Company simply could not satisfy demand. It was clear, to interested financial and political groups in London, that making the most of the new colonial opportunities meant importing ever more Africans, certainly more than the Royal African Company could provide. Moreover, interlopers, private traders, were increasingly successful in breaking the company's monopoly in supplying planters with Africans. To keep the slave trade exclusively in British hands, and to regulate it, Navigation Acts had been passed (between the 1650s and the 1670s), the whole system monitored by courts in the Americas and enforced by an increasingly powerful Royal Navy in the Atlantic and Caribbean. But how could a single company secure a trading monopoly over such a vast area of trade, spanning the African slave coast, the Atlantic shipping lanes and the myriad islands of the Caribbean?

The initial trading company, founded in 1663, had, within a decade, secured a string of African trading posts stretching from Senegambia to Benin. In 1672, the business was restructured as the Royal African Company. The company shipped an average of 5,250 Africans across the Atlantic each year, mainly in the 1680s. By 1713, when the company's monopoly was ended, it had transported a total of 120,000 Africans. Even such a large number of Africans was not enough to satisfy the planters. Moreover, long before then, *most* Africans landing in British colonies came not from the Royal African Company but from private traders. Put simply, free trade had won against restriction and monopoly. The end result was that by 1700 the British had carried more Africans as slaves than any other European nation. But what followed, over the next century, was even more astonishing (Map 26).

In the 145 years between 1662 and 1807, British ships carried 3.25 million Africans across the Atlantic. The Africans were drawn from a vast coastline: from Senegambia in the north to south of the River Congo. The numbers from these regions were 246,800 from Senegambia, 483,100 from Sierra Leone, 509,200 from the Gold Coast, 359,600 from the Bight of Benin and, most of all, 1,172,800 from the Bight of Biafra. From West Central Africa, the British shipped 634,000 Africans. Despite these concentrations, throughout the eighteenth century Europeans trawled for slaves along much of the West African coastline, though the British, with trading posts in Sierra Leone, Gambia, the Gold Coast and later in Old and New Calabar, tended to remain uninterested in what they called Angola, the region effectively controlled by the Portuguese. Like all other Europeans, the British gave the outward appearance of security on the coast, in their slave forts and factories. In fact, they had little more than a toehold on the African coast. In some places they developed secure permanent settlements, working with local African communities, indeed becoming, through racial and family mix, *part* of those communities. Elsewhere (and much depended on geography) they traded from forts, from factories, from encampments, on beaches, from riverside locations or from their own ships offshore, ferrying Africans back and forth between the ships riding at anchor in the Atlantic or in the river. Whatever the location, the ascendant British slave traders gathered Africans wherever they could find them, acquiring handfuls at different places, sailing from one spot to another, until the captain had decided that he had enough Africans below decks to make profitable business and turned the ship into the trade winds to sail west to the Americas.

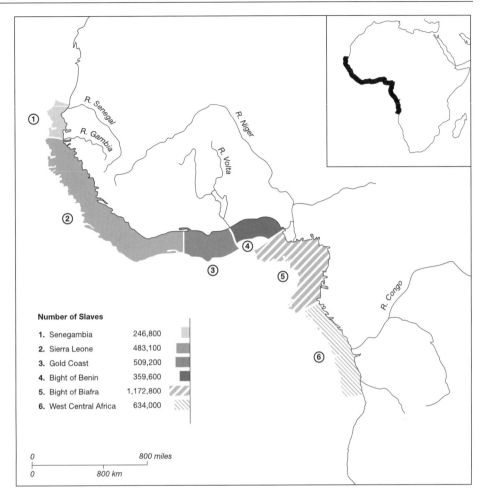

Number of Slaves

1. Senegambia	246,800	
2. Sierra Leone	483,100	
3. Gold Coast	509,200	
4. Bight of Benin	359,600	
5. Bight of Biafra	1,172,800	
6. West Central Africa	634,000	

Map 26 Shipment of slaves from West Africa in British Empire ships, 1662–1807
Source: After Marshall, P. J. (ed.) (1998) *The Oxford History of the British Empire: Volume II: The Eighteenth Century*, Map 20.1, p. 443. By permission of Oxford University Press.

The Atlantic slave trade thus became a massive industry. It was also an industry that spawned a complexity of other businesses and trades throughout the Atlantic world. It became, in effect, the lubricant of a huge Atlantic trading system, and it reminds us of the need, throughout, to integrate the slave trade with the wider commercial activities of which the slave trade was a critical part. By the third quarter of the eighteenth century, for example, £2,750,000 worth of British exports were shipped to British slave colonies in the Americas annually. In return, Britain received annual imports from its West Indian slave colonies alone of £3,150,000. West Africa shipped £77,000 worth of goods annually direct to Britain by the mid-eighteenth century. But the figures for the slave trade were the most striking of all Atlantic statistics. By the last quarter of the seventeenth century, the British were shipping 6,700 Africans each year; a century later, that figure had risen to more than 40,000 annually. There were dips and breaks in the pattern, determined by warfare (a regular occurrence in the

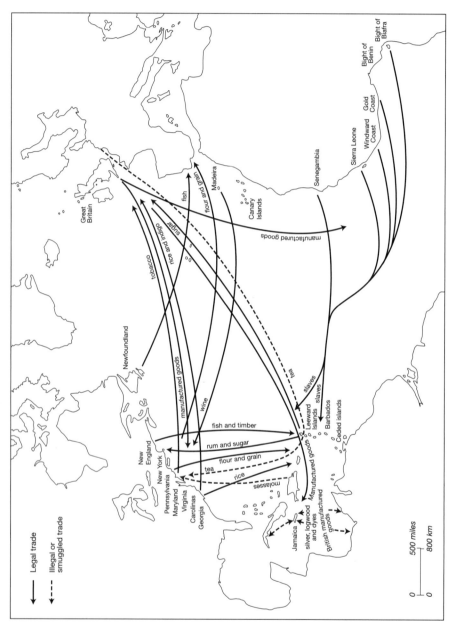

Map 27 The British North Atlantic trading system, c. 1768–1772

Source: After Porter, A. (ed.) (1991) *Atlas of British Overseas Expansion*, Routledge, p. 45.

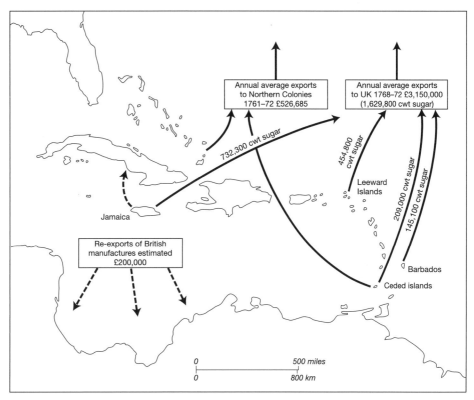

Annual average exports
to Northern Colonies
1761–72 £526,685

Annual average exports
to UK 1768–72 £3,150,000
(1,629,800 cwt sugar)

732,300 cwt sugar

454,800 cwt sugar

Leeward
Islands

209,000 cwt sugar

145,100 cwt sugar

Jamaica

Re-exports of British
manufactures estimated
£200,000

Barbados

Ceded islands

0   500 miles
0   800 km

Map 28 Exports from the West Indies: annual averages, 1768–1772
Source: After Porter, A. (ed.) (1991) *Atlas of British Overseas Expansion*, Routledge, p. 49.

eighteenth century) and by changes in demand in the Americas, but in the century and a half prior to abolition in 1807, the British transported more Africans than any other slaving nation.

Throughout the history of the British slaving industry, the *domestic* centre of trading interests shifted from London to Bristol, then to Liverpool, though a large number of other British ports also joined in, notably Glasgow in the tobacco trade, sending local ships to Africa for slaves, hence to the Americas for barter, commodities and exchange. Throughout, London remained critical for finance and insurance in this as in all other forms of overseas trade and finance (Maps 27–30).

The explosive growth in trade in African humanity was nourished by the labour demands of the American plantations, especially in sugar, tobacco and rice cultivation, but the apparently endless supplies of Africans arriving at docksides throughout the Americas can only *partly* be explained by labour demand on the plantations. After all, 90 percent of all Africans destined for the slave ships were sold by other Africans. And here lies a curiosity. Planters in the Americas were, on the whole, keen to buy healthy young males. Slave traders too wanted healthy young African males to load into their ships (in order to make profitable trade at slave sales in the Americas). But how could internal African forces, propelling captives towards the European ships on the coast, be

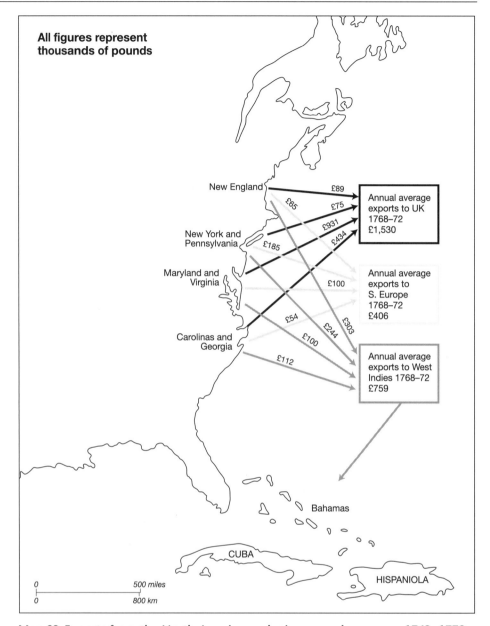

All figures represent thousands of pounds

New England

New York and Pennsylvania

Maryland and Virginia

Carolinas and Georgia

£89

£65

£75

£931

£434

£185

£100

£54

£244

£303

£100

£112

Annual average exports to UK 1768–72 £1,530

Annual average exports to S. Europe 1768–72 £406

Annual average exports to West Indies 1768–72 £759

Bahamas

CUBA

HISPANIOLA

0   500 miles
0   800 km

Map 29 Exports from the North American colonies: annual averages, 1768–1772
Source: After Shepherd, J. F. and Walton, G. M. (1972) *Shipping, Maritime Trade and the Economic Development of Colonial North America*, Cambridge University Press, p. 94.

responsive to the demands of slavers and planters on the far side of the Atlantic? Out of sight of Europeans on the slave ships, clearly there were complicated forces at work inside Africa: forces over which outsiders (notably European slave traders and American planters) had little say or control. Was the supply of Africans a result of what was happening in Africa itself? Can the Atlantic slave trade be explained by Africa – and not by the Americas?

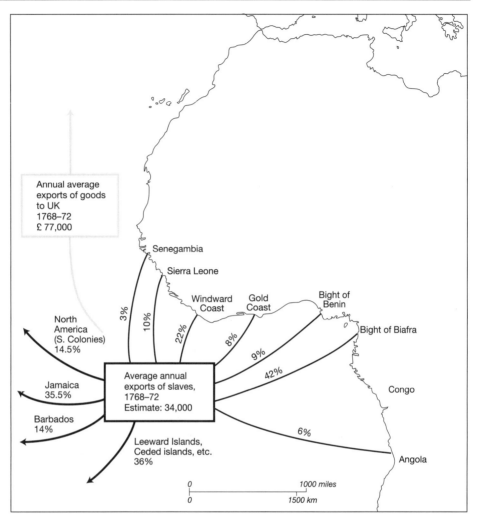

Map 30 British exports from West Africa: annual averages, 1768–1772
Source: After Porter, A. (ed.) (1991) *Atlas of British Overseas Expansion*, Routledge, p. 50.

CHAPTER 8

Africa

The first European slave traders on the coast were little more than pirates, happy to seize Africans they encountered and bundle them on board for return to Spain, Portugal or the Atlantic islands. However, such actions were counter-productive and could never form the basis for a permanent trade. What slavers needed, and what developed, were trading and commercial links with Africans on the coast. In their turn, African coastal traders and middlemen required commercial links with other Africans inland. Long before the arrival of Euro-peans slavers, there were well-established trading links between coastal peoples and African societies in the interior. In the 'age of exploration', Europeans made contact with a host of existing trading systems, flows of human migrations and oceanic trading links in all parts of the world: in North America, in Asia and in Africa. The gold that was a key attraction drawing Europeans to the African coast came, not from the coast itself, but from gold fields in the interior (Map 22). The same pattern emerged in the slave trade, as growing European demand for African slaves, at first for the Iberian peninsula and the Atlantic islands, tapped into existing African trading routes.

From the first, Europeans could not control or dictate the nature and number, or the flow and patterns, of Africans arriving as slaves on the coast. Moreover, few Europeans wanted to linger on the coast itself. West Africa quickly estab-lished a reputation as a dangerous region where whites failed to survive for very long. Europeans faced hostile environments in all corners of the globe in the course of their travels and colonizations, and they experienced ferocious levels of sickness and mortality globally, but in the words of Philip Curtin, 'tropical Africa falls into a category all its own'. The slave traders' ideal was to trade, load the ship and leave as soon as possible, but the expansion of the slave trade among all major European powers led to the establishment of permanent Euro-pean bases – most spectacularly in the form of slave forts, some of which survive to this day. The forts were permanent, but their European residents tended to be short-lived or transient.

However, there were groups of racially mixed peoples, part European, part African (notably in Portuguese settlements), which developed into established trading communities. Occasionally, they emerged as major commercial dynas-ties, with family branches and trading links on both sides of the Atlantic. None-theless, the general rule is clear enough: that Africa was a hostile environment for Europeans, a fact most readily measured in the mortality figures suffered by white crews on the slave ships trading on the coast, which reached extraordin-ary levels. A death rate of 15 percent *per month* has been measured on 1,535 French slave ships. On Liverpool ships in the 1770s, 20 percent died on the Atlantic crossing, but the figure was 45 percent per month when ships were on the African coast.

The supply of Africans destined for the European ships on the coast remained in the hands of African dealers. It was they who moved the coffles of slaves from the point of enslavement to the traders on the coast. The captives often passed through many hands, crossing great distances, often down Africa's major river systems, before reaching the coast. There were important trading and governing elites in West and Central Africa making profitable trade in supplying Africans, initially to other Africans, finally to Europeans. The basic point is simple enough. The internal slave trade – the flow of Africans from the African interior to the coast – was in the hands of Africans. European slave traders acquired the very great majority of all the slaves destined for the Americas from other Africans.

Slavery had been a feature of many African societies long before the Europeans arrived by sea. Indeed, Europeans first encountered Africans in the Mediterranean as a result of indigenous African slave systems. Moreover, it was the *existence* of slavery in Africa that enabled Europeans to accept Africans as slaves in the first place, acquiring them in their early ventures as part of their broader trading relationship with Africans. Existing slave systems within Africa were clearly a critical element in the development of Atlantic slavery, but it is also true that the arrival of the Europeans by sea, and the demand for slaves generated by the American plantations, had a transforming effect on slavery within Africa.

Early Europeans encountered, and did business with, African coastal elites that were already major collectors of, and traders in, slaves from the interior. Those slaves came mainly from warfare, which followed political upheavals caused by the fragmenting of major African states, notably Ghana, Mali and Songhai (Map 31). In response to growing European demand for more slaves, coastal elites readily devised slaving ventures directed at vulnerable interior states. In addition, regular supplies of African slaves were produced by belligerent Central African states, notably Kongo, whose violence yielded prisoners for onward sale to Europeans (Map 32). The European traders quickly adapted themselves to existing African slaving systems, but in their turn, Africans soon appreciated what Europeans required, i.e. more and more African slaves.

Slaves were recruited largely via warfare, between feuding states and empires (though both tended to be much smaller than contemporary European versions), providing prisoners that became a form of wealth to Europeans and to the African enslavers alike. The arrival of the Europeans, naturally enough, greatly accentuated demand for slaves, though not all African societies complied with these outside demands: some societies simply refused to become involved in slave trading. After 1650, however, the massive expansion of Atlantic slavery to populate the plantations had enormous consequences for Africa. In some regions (notably Angola), it seems to have retarded the growth of the local population. In this confusion of migrations of people, slavery may also have shifted diseases into new environments. Some African states (in Senegal and Nigeria for example) simply collapsed in the confusion. Others, especially the Ashante people on the Gold Coast and in Dahomey, rose to prominence on the tides of warfare and slave trading (Map 33). For successful African slave-trading states, slavery generated commercial wealth and political strength. In addition to all this, the voracious

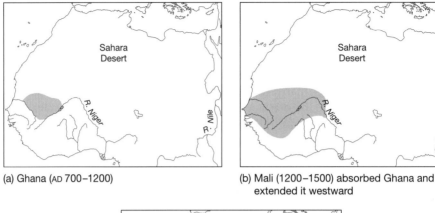

(a) Ghana (AD 700–1200)

(b) Mali (1200–1500) absorbed Ghana and extended it westward

(c) Songhai (1350–1600) slowly usurped the territory of Mali

Map 31 Major African empires between the eighth and sixteenth centuries
Source: After Davidson, B. (1966) *African Kingdoms*, Time Life Books, p. 81.

European appetite for slaves prompted an increase in slavery *within* Africa itself. The use of slaves among Africans seems to have expanded because of slavery in the Atlantic. Thus what seems, at first glance, to be a transfer of slaves to Europeans on the coast was just the most visible (to Europeans) of huge slaving systems that stretched deep into Africa itself. The European coastal presence had massive and far-reaching consequences throughout West and Central Africa. Given the numbers of people involved, how could it have been otherwise?

For the millions of Africans involved, sale to white men, and the brutal loading on to the slave ships, was only the latest in a long line of humiliating transactions. From their initial point of enslavement deep in the interior they had been passed from hand to hand, from one African slaver to another, often for months at a time. Some sold in the Bight of Biafra, for instance, had travelled perhaps only 100 kilometres, whereas others (the Bambara destined for Louisiana, and those travelling from Angola to Brazil) had travelled great distances to the coast from the interior. The journeys travelled, normally on foot, and the physical toll that they took of the slaves, added to the overall distress suffered by the millions of Africans involved – and all *before* they arrived at the slave ships.

On the coast, slaves were sold and bartered in return for a great range of imported European goods (and other items transshipped through Europe from

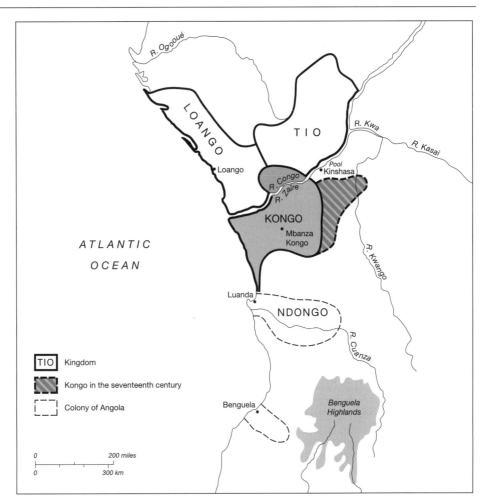

Map 32 Kongo and Angola, sixteenth and seventeenth centuries
Source: After Curtin, P. D. *et al.* (1978) *African History*, Longman, p. 228.

Asia). The prolonged negotiating sessions (all lubricated with drink and gifts) between European traders and the African middlemen, local rulers and traders saw cargoes of varied goods pass into African hands, and thence into the interior: luxuries and essentials, metal goods, arms, drink, textiles, cowrie shells. Prominent Africans on the coast acquired a taste for the basics and, increasingly, for the luxuries of the Western world. In return, they handed over the batches of African slaves, each with his/her own value depending on age, health and sex. It was a process common to many other slave trades: in medieval Europe or in the trans-Sahara trade.

There is one simple (but often unasked) question that lies behind this massive, brutal system. Why ship millions of Africans across the Atlantic if tropical and subtropical crops could have been grown in West Africa? Why not develop tropical agriculture where labour was abundant – Africa – rather than ship that labour at great cost across the Atlantic? The answer is simple enough. Europeans did not survive long in the hostile climate of West Africa. It is also clear that

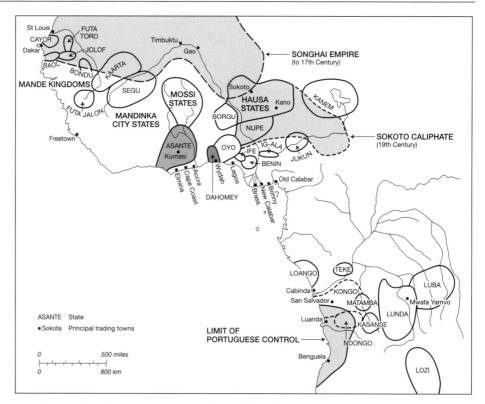

Map 33 West African states and principal trading towns
Source: After *Dictionary of Afro-American Slavery* edited by R. M. Miller and J. D. Smith. Copyright © 1988 by Randall M. Miller and John David Smith. Reproduced with permission of Greenwood Publishing Group, Inc., Westport, CT.

sugar (the crop that absorbed 70 percent of all slaves) was more suited to the tropical Americas than West Africa. Nonetheless, the key fact is that Europeans were not safe in West Africa. They were in effect temporary figures on the African coastline. Moreover, they could not have filled their slave ships without the help and cooperation of Africans. At every step in what became a protracted business, Europeans were dependent on Africans and had to negotiate and barter for the purchase of slaves from Africans on the coast.

Both sides were nervously wary of each other, worried that negotiations could break down, that gestures and reactions might be misunderstood and that the whole affair might disintegrate into violence. Throughout, slavery was a violent institution and Europeans were permanently alert to its inherent dangers, protecting themselves on their ships, and on land, against African dangers. At the point of face-to-face contact between Europeans and Africans, business dealings were often fraught with cultural problems and misunderstandings, and violence was rarely far away. Both sides might, and often did, resort to violence when understanding broke down. Europeans raided African communities and took hostages; Africans took over European ships.

The coastal slave trade was hardly a trade between equals. Europeans might have superior firepower, but that was no guarantee of safety. Africans played

Europeans off one against another, and Europeans could impose their military power no further than their guns could fire, from ship or fort. The forts looked impressive, but Europeans were ultimately marooned in them: hemmed in by the ocean on one side and Africa on the other. At every point, European slave traders were unable to impose firm control or a dominant presence in Africa itself – a central fact that persisted well into the nineteenth century.

One simple consequence of this was that, if they wanted Africans to work for them in the tropics, it had to be *outside* Africa itself. Thus it was that an industry in humanity evolved that saw, in time, twelve million Africans loaded on to the slave ships destined for the Americas. All this was made possible not simply by the European presence on the coast but also by the continuing involvement of complex slaving systems in the African interior. Africans enslaved and sold each other. However, it would be wrong to view this as Africans selling 'fellow Africans'. They were enslaving and selling other, different people. The concept of being an 'African' had no meaning for the people involved. The terms 'African' and 'Africa' were European terms that, late in the eighteenth century, came to be used by politically active blacks on both sides of the Atlantic, but they had initially acquired the concept from Europeans. Throughout the era of the Atlantic slave trade, Africans had no more sense of being African (as opposed to a specific form of kin, language group or tribe) than a contemporary Yorkshireman might have felt himself to be a European.

In addition, the idea that enslavement of other alien people was wrong was largely unknown – in Europe or Africa – in these years of colonial expansion. When the idea began to gain ground in the late eighteenth century, it represented a new and quite revisionary mode of thought. As uncomfortable as it may seem today, enslavement of outsiders went unquestioned and unchallenged in all but a few cases. Africans felt no more uneasy about enslaving other Africans, from different cultures, than European traders felt uneasy when buying Africans on the coast.

However, slaves were not the sole African export. Until roughly 1700, the total value of gold and other commodities exported from West Africa was higher than the value of exported slaves. Thereafter, and spearheaded by the British, the exports of African slaves became *the* dominant African export into the Atlantic economy. In all forms of trade from West Africa, Africans played a critical role. Whether the trade on the coast was for gold or humanity, it was a trade that passed from African to European hands. It was a costly, and in some respects, an inefficient trading system, quite unlike any other form of trade established by Europeans in other parts of the globe. Yet it yielded the desired results and made possible the transit of twelve million Africans into the slave ships and the eventual arrival of the weakened and traumatized survivors in the Americas.

CHAPTER 9

The Atlantic

The Atlantic slave trade, like all seaborne movements of people in the age of sail, depended on natural forces that were beyond the power of man to control but that he might, with experience and good fortune, learn to use and master. Europeans developed two distinct sailing routes to the Americas, both determined by nature. The first, across the North Atlantic, the other sailing south and west towards tropical America.

In the former, Europeans began by working the abundant fisheries off Canada; in the latter, they developed their plantation colonies (where they fed the slaves on salt fish imported from northern waters). Once European sailors had become familiar with the quirks of the Atlantic, the ocean made its own impact on subsequent European and African development of the Americas. Its currents and prevailing winds directed the specific flow of maritime traffic: from Africa to the Americas, into the Caribbean and north to North America, northeastwards from the Caribbean and back to Europe. Even the seasonality of maritime trade was affected by the weather: ships needed to clear the West Indies before midsummer and the onset of the hurricane season (Maps 34–36).

Trial and error provided vital training for sailors in the Atlantic. The initial sailing experience of adventurous fishermen in the waters off Canada added to the accumulating European experience of oceanic crossings and was useful on later voyages. Spaniards were prominent among the early fishermen in the North Atlantic, but perhaps the greatest of Spanish discoveries was how the mix of current and tide would carry them direct to tropical America. Key features of Spanish America were defined in large measure by the nature of their sailing ventures. The normal pattern was that they departed Seville and Cadiz for the Canaries, thence catching the trade winds and the northern equatorial current across the Atlantic, entering the Caribbean via the Mona or Dominica passage, to Santo Domingo. From there, it was a direct route to Vera Cruz or Nombre de Dios on the isthmus of Panama, later Portobello. There, Spanish vessels made *rendezvous* with goods and people travelling to and from Peru and Mexico. Wintering in Havana on the way home, the Spanish fleets joined the Gulf Stream in the Straits of Florida before heading east towards the Azores and thence to Spain. The treasure fleets – loaded with riches beyond imagination plundered from Mexico and Peru – inevitably attracted French and English privateers, forcing the Spanish to develop the major fortifications at San Juan, Cartagena, Havana and Santo Domingo and to travel home in armed convoys (Map 37). By the end of the sixteenth century, Europeans were fighting each other for the rich pickings, the secure bases and the produce of their early ventures in tropical America.

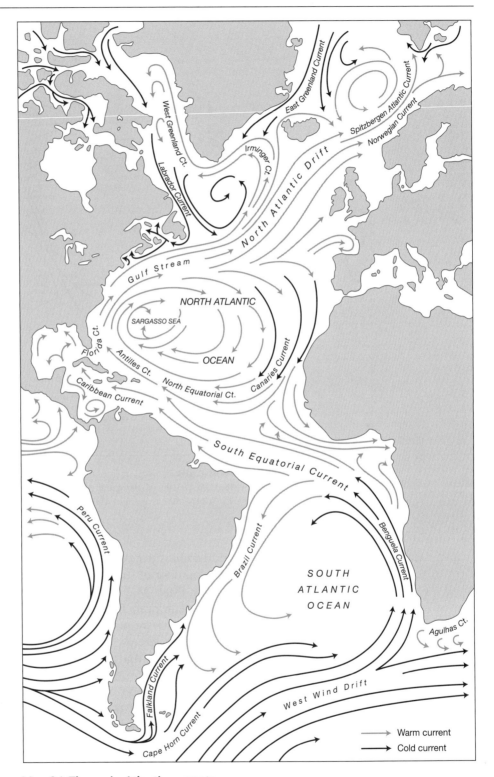

Map 34 The main Atlantic currents

Source: Adapted from *The English Atlantic, 1675–1740: An Exploration of Communication and Community* by Ian K. Steele, copyright © 1986 by Ian K. Steele. Used by permission of Oxford University Press, Inc.

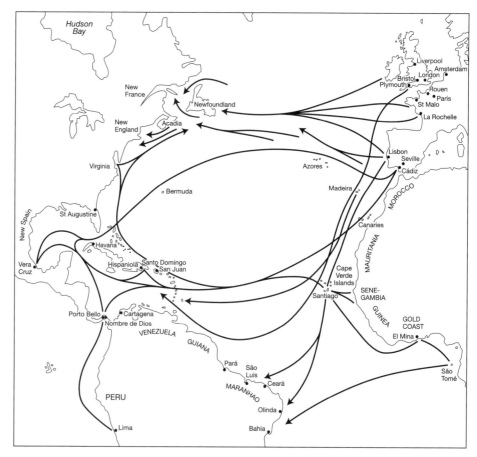

Map 35 Major Atlantic sailing routes
Source: After Meinig, D. W. (1986) *The Shaping of America: a geographical perspective on 500 years of history. Volume 1: Atlantic America, 1492–1800*, Copyright 1986 Yale University, Yale University Press, p. 56.

Something like one hundred ships per year returned with American produce and treasures before the development of sugar in Brazil opened a new Atlantic axis via the Cape Verde Islands (Map 38). All three transatlantic systems were linked by their dependence on European finance (based in Antwerp initially, later in Amsterdam), but Europeans were permanently divided by conflicts between national and commercial self-interests, and they began that squabbling antagonism in all corners of the globe that was to characterize their histories throughout the colonial years.

In Africa, as we have seen, European bases on the coast and rivers were linked to the existing internal trading systems of the African interior, most of which were utterly transformed by the development of the European trading presence on the coast and by the growth of slavery in the Americas. The most obvious outcome was the creation of utterly new communities in the Americas that were largely African, though moderated by local (indigenous Indian) and European influences. Those black communities were also shaped by the experience of

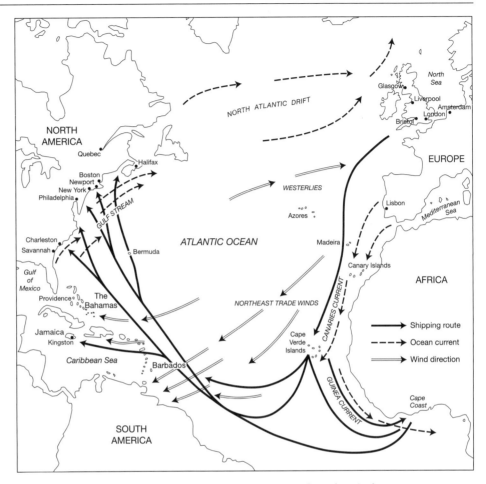

Map 36 Atlantic shipping routes, ocean currents and trade winds
Source: Benjamin, Thomas, Timothy D. Hall and David E. Rutherford, *The Atlantic World in the Age of Empire*. Copyright © 2001 by Houghton Mifflin Company. Adapted with permission.

oceanic travel and trade. Slave societies across the Americas needed maritime links to the outside world, at first for their simple survival, later for their material well-being. They were sustained by more and more Africans arriving from the slave ships, and food and hardware from the shipping routes direct to and from North America and Europe. To complete the cycle, the slave system could only survive in the tropical Americas by the export of produce cultivated by the strength and skills of imported Africans and their European supervisors. It was an integrated whole: an Atlantic economy that fused together the peoples, the lands and the produce of three vast and widely separated continents. And all were linked by the vagaries of oceanic life on the Atlantic.

The Atlantic weather systems dictated the ebb and flow of mankind and produce within the enslaved Atlantic. The first European arrival on the West African coast had been held up by contemporary limitations of European navigation and seamanship (and by fears of the unknown). The physical condition of Europeans on the African coast (their death rates and levels of sickness) was

**Map 37 The Americas: principal Spanish and Portuguese settlements
in the sixteenth and seventeenth centuries**
Source: After Phillips, W. D. (1985) *Slavery from Roman Times to the Early Atlantic Slave Trade*,
University of Minnesota Press.

largely determined by the length of time that Europeans were obliged to linger
there. The same was true – but worse – for those Africans penned below decks
on the coast, but their problems worsened as the ships headed out into the
Atlantic. It is clear enough now that one critical factor behind Africans' seaborne
miseries (death, disease and long-term trauma) was the length of time they
spent at sea. And that was often in the laps of the Atlantic gods. There were
marked differences in the speed of Atlantic crossings. European nations used
different-sized ships and experienced different crossing times. The French, for
example, were generally faster, largely because they used different-sized vessels.
British slave ships were among the smallest of all ocean-going vessels of the
period, yet they took longer to cross the Atlantic than their French and Dutch
rivals. But it is also true that Atlantic sailing times became shorter over time.

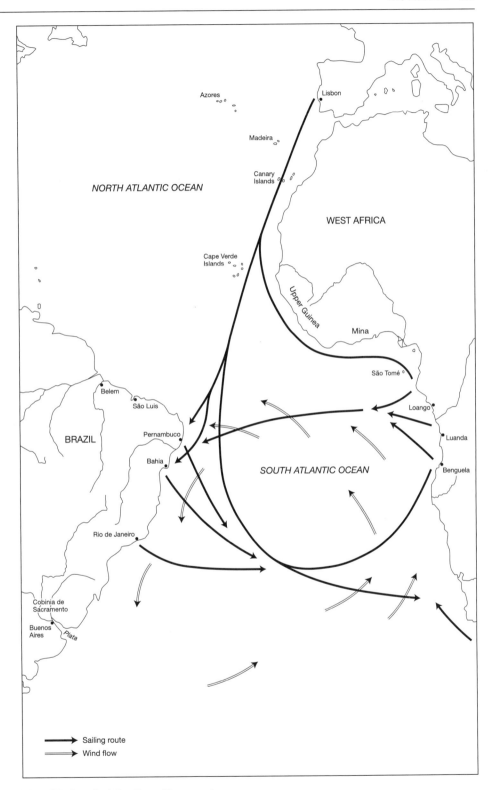

Map 38 South Atlantic sailing routes
Source: After Miller, Joseph C. *Way of Death.* © 1988. Reprinted by permission of The University of Wisconsin Press.

Obviously, they differed greatly depending on the points of departure and arrival, and the distances travelled.

From first to last European slave traders were in the business of making money. It was in their interest to get as many Africans as possible safely, and healthily, across the Atlantic. But their ability to do so was limited by natural forces over which they had so little control: the disease environment of West Africa; and the prevailing winds, currents and volatile weather systems of the Atlantic and the Caribbean. All this was in addition to the ubiquitous political, physical and military threats, in Africa, on board ship and on the high seas and in the Americas. Resistant Africans on the coast, dangerous slaves below decks, piratical or warring European rivals, all and more were ever-present realities to add to the natural and unavoidable dangers of long-distance oceanic travel in the age of sail in the Atlantic. That thousands of voyages persisted in the trade over so long a period is itself testimony to the lucrative prospects offered by Atlantic slavery.

CHAPTER 10

Crossing the Atlantic

About twelve million Africans began the Atlantic crossing – the Middle Passage – by being loaded into the slave ships, but only ten and a half million lived to see landfall on the far side of the Atlantic. All the Atlantic voyages were accompanied by sickness and death, which originated even before the slaves stepped on board, for most had been force-marched, often great distances, from the spot of their initial, violent enslavement. Though slave traders chose slaves carefully, they inevitably acquired sick and traumatized captives. Sick Africans could – and did – cause havoc when loaded into the holds.

Africans died on board as the ships traded on the coast, even before their floating prisons headed into the Atlantic. As the numbers of slaves in the holds increased, the physical management of sick, resentful and potentially rebellious Africans became more and more difficult for the crew. White sailors, always greatly outnumbered, were themselves exposed to the health risks of West Africa. Now, in close, intimate contact with large numbers of Africans, the health of everyone on board, black and white, became (along with physical security) the most pressing matter of shipboard life.

It was a brutal system, but the violence and humiliation meted out to the Africans when they arrived on board, the universal intimidation, the individual threats and the sheer terror of being loaded into a foetid and increasingly crowded hold of a ship in the tropics can deflect us from a simple point. The *purpose* of this violent system was profit. And there was no profit to be had from dead or disabled Africans. However high the mortality rates, however cruel the management of the slaves, the sole purpose was to make profitable trade in African humanity. Slave deaths cut into the slavers' profits. Slavers did not intend or plan to harm or kill their human cargoes. Quite the opposite. For all the contrary examples (of homicidal captains or barbarically savage crew members), the aim was to ship Africans as quickly as possible in healthy (i.e. sellable) condition to the slave markets of the Americas. Nonetheless, despite changes, the Atlantic slave trade was brutal for all, fatal for many. For its sheer human misery it was, in the words of David Eltis, 'unrivalled before, during, and after the era of the transatlantic slave trade'. Other shipping experiences offer comparisons of human suffering: indentured and convict labour in the seventeenth and eighteenth centuries, for example. But whichever example we study, the slave experience was worse on every index of comparison. They were more crowded (even though 'packing' of slaves became less dense with time), more of them fell sick, and more of them died. The density of travellers on other ships to the West Indies in the late seventeenth century was less than *one-sixth* that experienced by African slaves. Even when we examine the worst experience of convict or military transportation in the age of sail, the data of human misery come nowhere near the levels of suffering endured by the slaves. They were, in short, subjected to a more brutal regime than any other oceanic travellers in the modern age.

The raw figures – the data – for the Atlantic slave trade leave perhaps the most striking and indelible of impressions: twelve million captives, ten and a half million survivors, some 27,000 known slave voyages, 12,000 of which were British or British colonial between 1699 and 1807 – and 5,000 of which came from Liverpool. However, figures can deflect us from a simple fact: that such data are merely a statistical representation of vast human suffering.

A clear majority of African slaves were men, though the sex ratio varied from time to time. More than that, the total number of Africans overwhelmed the numbers of Europeans migrating westwards. It is customary to think that the Americas were settled by migrating Europeans, but the numbers of white migrants were dwarfed by the number of African slaves. Up to the 1820s – after which Europe began to unleash millions of its poor – some 2.4 million Europeans had crossed the Atlantic, but in the same period, 8.4 million Africans were transported in the slave ships. In time, Africans and their descendants were to be found scattered across the Americas, but the overwhelming majority were initially destined for the tropics and subtropics: for Brazil and the Caribbean. Fewer than 10 percent of the total were delivered to North America.

As the transatlantic slave voyages became commonplace, the routines of sailing developed established patterns. Different nations had their favourite destinations, but everyone was at the mercy of the elements, and the main shipping lanes were determined, in the age of sail, by prevailing winds and currents. Slavers wanted a speedy crossing, but much depended on their point of departure. Ships leaving the northern slave-trading region of Senegambia reached their destinations in 48+ days: ships from the more southerly slaving coasts took more than 70 days. Atlantic crossing times varied hugely, though they became shorter as the trade developed. The average time to Brazil was one month, and two months to the Caribbean and North America.

As the time for the crossing decreased, the size of the slave ships increased, enabling the larger ships to carry more slaves per voyage. By the late eighteenth century, English ships were carrying 390 Africans, the French and Portuguese an average of 340. In the nineteenth century, in the era of the 'illegal' slave trade to Brazil and Cuba, Portuguese slave ships were shipping Africans in the high 400s. However, there was an exception to this rule about increasing ship size and slave numbers: slave ships to North America remained small. In the mid-eighteenth century, they carried an average of 200 Africans. After Acts of Parliament in 1788 and 1799 (a response to mounting abolitionist pressures in Britain), British slavers had their capacity regulated, and in the last decade of the British slave trade, the average number of Africans in British ships fell to 289.

The levels of slave mortality on those slave ships varied enormously. Longer voyages, or virulent disease, inevitably raised the death rates. Up to the early seventeenth century, death rates ran at an average of 20 percent. By the late eighteenth century, however, slave deaths on the Atlantic crossing had dropped to half that level, and by the end of the slave trade very few slave ships experienced the high levels of slave deaths common in the earlier period. This fall in slave mortality was common to all European and American slave traders.

Today, historians have come to accept that slave deaths on the ships were partly a reflection of health problems brought on to the ships from Africa. African diseases, political upheavals, famine (with its impact on prisoners/slaves) – all clearly affected the individual and communal health of the Africans loaded into the slave ships on the coast. There were, it is true, efforts to regulate the slave trade, with national legislation insisting that Africans were shipped in less onerous conditions, but such changes, with a few exceptions, did little to affect mortality. Feeding, watering, cleaning and exercising the slaves improved, but such improvements came about more via trial and error.

Though slave ships were bigger by the late eighteenth century than previously, they were smaller than other contemporary ships engaged in oceanic trade. Slave ships were also designed differently, notably being better ventilated. Experience taught slavers to carry food and water for *twice* the expected crossing time, but sometimes mistakes were made – with catastrophic consequences for the Africans, none more grotesque than the infamous *Zong* massacre, when the captain of the Liverpool slaver the *Zong* ditched 130+ Africans overboard when he ran short of supplies (in the hope of recouping the loss on insurance).

The death rates on the slave ships were not as high as many have claimed, but they never fell below 5 percent – and that was among a group of largely younger people. Slaves died primarily from gastro-intestinal illnesses, the main one being the 'bloody flux', itself a consequence of the stable-like filth in the holds (made worse by bad weather). Ailments carried on board from Africa accounted for other deaths. Disastrous mortality levels were normally explained by shipboard epidemics but slave traders were also acutely aware that they might also lose slaves – and their own lives – to shipboard revolts. There are records of 493 revolts on slave ships, most taking place in the late eighteenth century. When shipboard slave revolts decreased in the nineteenth century, the slave trade itself had changed and had become essentially a trade in very young slaves and children.

The physical dangers to the Africans did not end with landfall in the Americas. As we shall see, most of the new arrivals faced a difficult period (of up to 18 months) settling in. Death rates in that 'seasoning period' were again high and need to be thought of as the last leg of the slave trade itself. Slaves were often transshipped from the arrival point. Almost 200,000 Africans were re-exported from Jamaica, mainly to Spanish and French colonies. The Dutch first landed their slaves in Curaçao before shipping them on to various Spanish possessions. Many Africans travelled across the isthmus thence south towards Colombia, while others crossed Panama and on to Lima. Africans landing in South America sometimes faced daunting onward journeys, normally on foot, through various climate zones and changes in elevation. Many landing in the Chesapeake had already been transshipped via the Caribbean, but even they might be moved on, into the interior of that vast river system. Not surprisingly, many Africans did not survive arrival in the Americas. We need, then, to be cautious about the statistics about death and sickness on the Atlantic crossing,

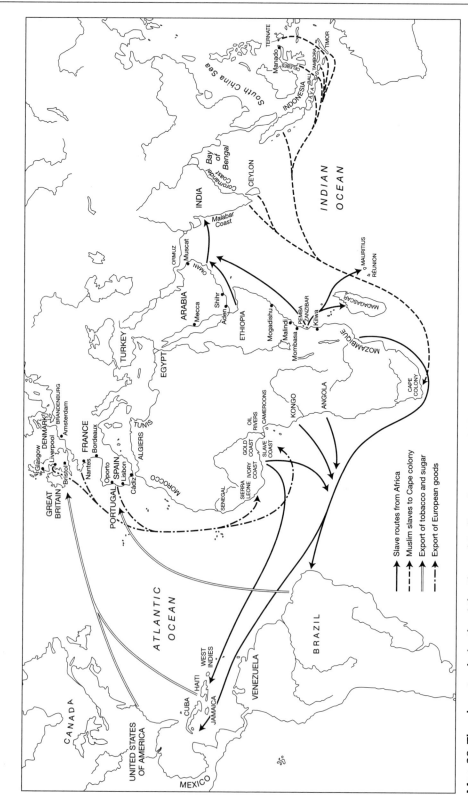

Map 39 The slave trade in the Atlantic and Indian Oceans, c. 1800

Source: After Freeman-Grenville, G. S. P. *The New Atlas of African History*, R. G. Collings.

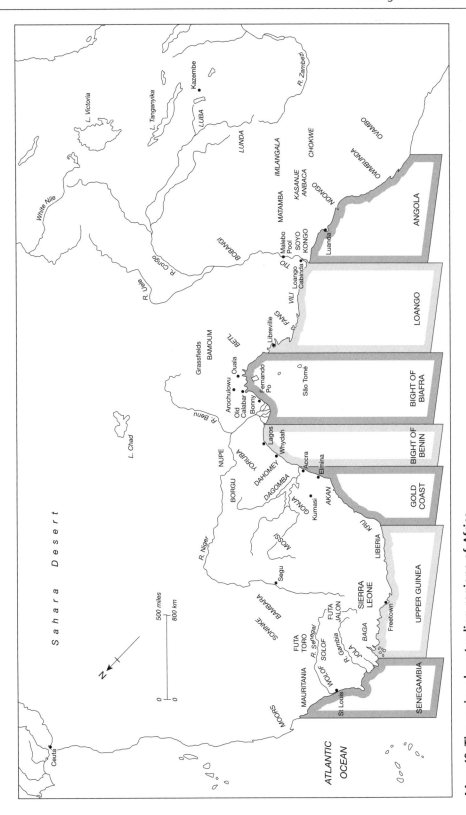

Map 40 The major slave-trading regions of Africa
Source: Adapted from Iliffe, J. (1995) *Africans: The History of a Continent*, Cambridge University Press, p. 128.

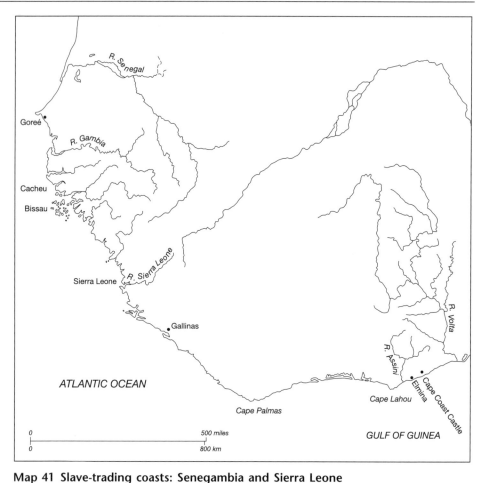

Map 41 Slave-trading coasts: Senegambia and Sierra Leone
Source: After Klein, H. S. (1999) *The Atlantic Slave Trade*, Cambridge University Press, p. xiv.

because the Africans' torments continued long *after* they stumbled off the slave
ships. It is clear that many Africans succumbed to their oceanic illnesses long
after they had left the ships behind them.

Though the Atlantic slave trade was eventually dominated by the British, it
attracted the major European (and American) maritime nations, all united in
one common purpose. They were all keen to transport enslaved Africans profitably into the Americas. Enormous risks were involved: bad weather, warfare,
disease on board, slave rebellion and violence, all and more added imponderables
to the dangerous task of sailing thousands of miles. Yet the fact that so many
nations, over so long a period, shipped unprecedented numbers of people is
itself testimony to the economic attractions of the Atlantic slave trade. The
maritime slave trade was abolished in 1807 by the British and the Americans
(earlier by the Danes), yet despite abolition an estimated three million Africans
were shipped across the Atlantic, mainly to Brazil and Cuba, *after* abolition. For
all its violence and terror, one dominant fact stands out in the history of the
Atlantic slave trade. In the words of Herbert Klein, 'the overwhelming majority

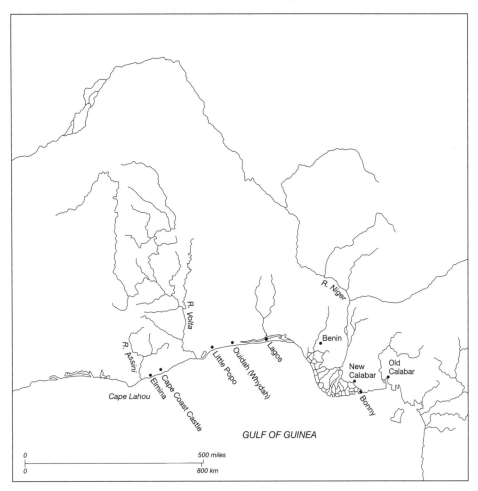

Map 42 Slave-trading coasts: the Gold Coast, and the Bights of Benin and Biafra
Source: After Klein, H. S. (1999) *The Atlantic Slave Trade*, Cambridge University Press, p. xv.

of the slaves did reach America'. This was, after all, the purpose of the slave trade and the main aim of the Atlantic traders.

The Atlantic crossings constituted the largest enforced movement of peoples known to the pre-twentieth-century world. Though the process of enslavement began deep in Africa and continued long after landfall in the Americas, it was the unique terrors of crossing the Atlantic that seem to have scarred the Africans most deeply. Not surprisingly, the Atlantic slave trade has come to symbolize the most brutal feature of the wider story of slavery in the Americas (Maps 39–42).

CHAPTER 11

Destinations

Africans were landed in a myriad places across the face of the Americas, from the Chesapeake region of North America, throughout the Caribbean and south to Brazil. The precise landfall and point of departure determined the length and nature of the Atlantic crossing. It was, for example, relatively quick to sail from Angola to Brazil, but to sail from Biafra to the Chesapeake took considerably longer, depending on currents, winds, seamanship – and luck.

The broad pattern of African arrivals in the Americas responded to local American demand and tells us where and when local slave labour was being used most intensively. Before 1600, for example (though the numbers were relatively small), Africans were shipped to Spanish America (the Caribbean, Mexico and the rest of Central America) and to Brazil. Some 75,000 were landed in Spanish America and 50,000 in Brazil. Over the next fifty years, those numbers destined for Spanish America and Brazil increased dramatically (largely because of the expansion of sugar), but the real explosion in African imports took place from the 1640s onwards. Those were the years of the development of the British and French Caribbean islands and the initial establishment of slavery in British North America. But it was the eighteenth century that witnessed the most impressive growth in African imports. Whereas in the sixty years before 1700 1.6 million Africans had been landed in the Americas, over the next century that figure increased to 6.4 million. And even in the next century, almost three million Africans were transported, mainly to Cuba and Brazil.

The establishment of the sugar industry in northeast Brazil prompted the major arrival of Africans. In 1570, there were perhaps 2,000–3,000 slaves in Brazil, rising to 10,000 by 1600. Over the next fifty years, some 100,000 Africans poured into that expansive sugar economy, which benefited from the decline of sugar cultivation on the Atlantic islands. Equally important, sugar could be shipped relatively quickly from northeast Brazil to the markets in Lisbon. By then, Africans were pouring into other settlements in the Americas: 50,000 to Spanish America, more than 20,000 into the newly settled British Caribbean islands (led by Barbados) and smaller numbers into the French islands. In the second half of the seventeenth century, perhaps 360,000 Africans were shipped into Brazil (Map 43; Klein, 210–11).

The very first Africans had been landed in Spanish America, often Spanish speakers from the Atlantic islands, and had accompanied the early Spanish explorations and settlements. The Spanish conquests proved disastrous for native Indian peoples, whose catastrophic decline was one factor behind the subsequent demand for imported Africans, but African imports into Spanish America remained relatively small, not least because Spanish attention quickly turned not so much

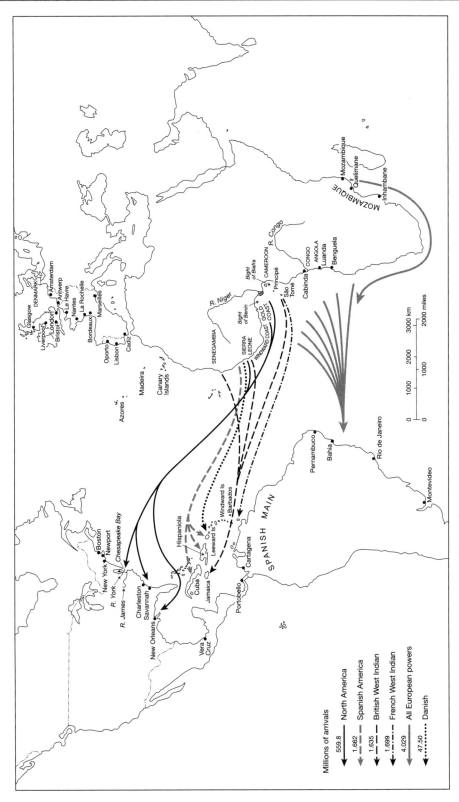

Map 43 African arrivals in the Americas, by region

Source: Adapted from Rawley, J. (1981) *Transatlantic Slave Trade: A History*, W. W. Norton & Company, p. xi, using data from Klein, H. S. (1999) *The Atlantic Slave Trade*, Cambridge University Press, p. 210.

to agriculture as to the fabled wealth of Central and South America. By the early seventeenth century, however, Portuguese slave traders were supplying many more Africans to Spanish possessions, though most were landed initially not in the islands but in Cartagena and Vera Cruz. By then, Africans had fanned out throughout the Spanish colonies to become a major component in most local populations. In 1610, half of Cuba's population consisted of slaves. In Lima in 1636, half the population was black, as it was in Mexico City. Moreover, the Spanish crown encouraged the slave trade because it benefited from licensing the trade. Though most of these early arrivals came via Portuguese traders, other European nations were drawn irresistibly towards the slave trade by its obvious potential for profit. By the end of the seventeenth century, Dutch, French and English traders (mainly privateers) had made sizeable inroads into the Atlantic slave trade. The Dutch, for example, by the mid-seventeenth century were shipping 2,500 Africans each year to Brazil (Klein, 77) though the Portuguese continued to transport upwards of 4,000 each year. The British had begun to transform the Atlantic slave trade in the late seventeenth century.

The arrival of the British heralded a shift in destinations, with ever more Africans being transported to the Caribbean and, on a much smaller scale, to British settlements in North America. The British addiction to African slaves began with the settlement in St Kitts (1624) and Barbados (1625) and the eventual conversion of Barbados to sugar. Between 1640 and 1700, about 134,500 Africans were shipped to Barbados; in the same period, the number of local whites began to fall. This process of Africanization in the Caribbean was even more dramatic when the British took Jamaica from Spain in 1655. Between 1660 and 1713, 160,548 Africans arrived in Jamaica on English ships. By 1713, English ships had carried about 400,000 Africans into the Americas (Eltis, 208).

From the mid-seventeenth century to the early eighteenth century, Barbados was the richest of the British colonies. The lessons learned in that small compact island (no bigger than the Isle of Wight) about money making on the back of Africans working in sugar were copied elsewhere, notably in Jamaica. But the islands settled by the British, including the small Leewards, were also important for the re-export of slaves to Spanish America. Before 1700, some 30,000 were shipped from Jamaica to Spanish colonies, and perhaps another 20,000 in the next thirteen years. Barbados similarly supplied smaller numbers of Africans to the Spanish. In the Leewards, the development of the local sugar industry encouraged the importation of slaves direct from Africa, though numbers had landed, initially in small batches, from Barbados and St Eustatius. The end result of all this was that by the early eighteenth century, the British Caribbean had become the major market for African slaves (Map 44).

There was a parallel development of tobacco production in the Chesapeake. The first Africans had been landed at Jamestown in 1619, but even as late as 1660 there were fewer than 2,000 blacks in the entire Chesapeake region. By 1713, however, more than 23,000 Africans had arrived (Eltis, 208). Over the following century, more than 100,000 were landed. Further south, the development of South Carolina was greatly influenced by migrants relocating from Barbados, and slavery thrived following the establishment of rice plantations. In the 1720s, perhaps 600 Africans a year were arriving in Charleston,

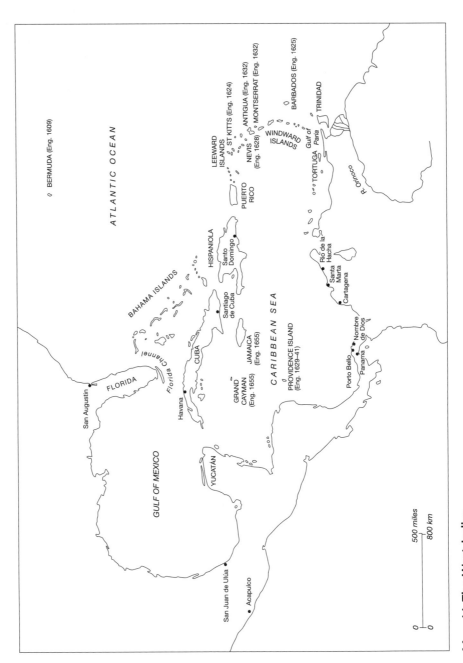

Map 44 The West Indies

Source: After Porter, A. (ed.) (1991) *Atlas of British Overseas Expansion*, Routledge, p. 25.

rising to 2,000 in the 1730s. By then there were perhaps 40,000 slaves in the region.

Arrival in the Americas may have meant an end to the slaves' seaborne sufferings, but there followed new, no less punishing regimes of physical torment. The Africans were mostly sick: they had no idea where they were, or what was about to happen to them. They had simply entered the next stage in the apparently (to them) unending round of sufferings – but this time in the alien world of the Americas.

CHAPTER 12

Arrivals

The slaves' Atlantic crossing had been an oceanic experience of unique terror. For most of their time at sea, the Africans were shackled below decks. Despite their ailments, they constituted too volatile and unpredictable a force to be allowed on deck unattended, except for short exercise periods in small groups (weather and manpower permitting). They had no idea what faced them at landfall. The Africans were destined for further sale, or for consignment to someone who had already put in a bid for them. This process also involved its own torments and indignities.

The Africans' experiences varied greatly from one American point of arrival to another, but the broad outlines remained similar. The largest numbers of Africans across the Atlantic were to Brazil and into the Caribbean, though the migrations to North America were much less numerous. In all cases, however, these main flows were dispersed, on arrival, from the main ports of entry into a myriad, onward routes by land and water. Brazil absorbed the largest number of Africans over the course of the Atlantic slave trade (some 4+ million; Klein, 210–11). Rio de Janeiro, the colonial capital after 1763, was the main Brazilian slave port from the seventeenth to the nineteenth century, though many other Africans arrived at Salvador and Recife. In Rio, newly arrived Africans were herded, sometimes in batches as large as 400, into slave warehouses, which were close to or part of merchants' houses. There they underwent physical inspection by potential buyers. But the unpleasantness of such large groups of (often sick) Africans close to local living quarters led to the development of designated slave baracoons: pens that were located an appropriate distance from complaining local residents. There, indeed everywhere in the Americas, on arrival the Africans were cleaned, fed and generally removed of their seaborne complaints and ailments (if possible) before they were sold on again. Potential buyers inspected the Africans, generally in the most intimate fashion, with the help of established, resident slaves who were familiar with the infirmities and problems of freshly arrived Africans. The new arrivals might be sold at auctions, and others were hawked around from place to place. New owners often branded their new slaves (Map 45).

The experiences of new arrivals varied enormously, depending largely on the point of arrival. Perhaps the most strenuous of all onward journeys were endured by Africans destined for one part of the Spanish empire, in Upper Peru (today's Bolivia). There, from the late sixteenth century onwards, Africans had been in demand for work in the mines and were marched inland from arrival on the Atlantic coast near Buenos Aires and on to the Andes. By 1750, Buenos Aires had become a major slave-trading port, and Africans, after recovery and

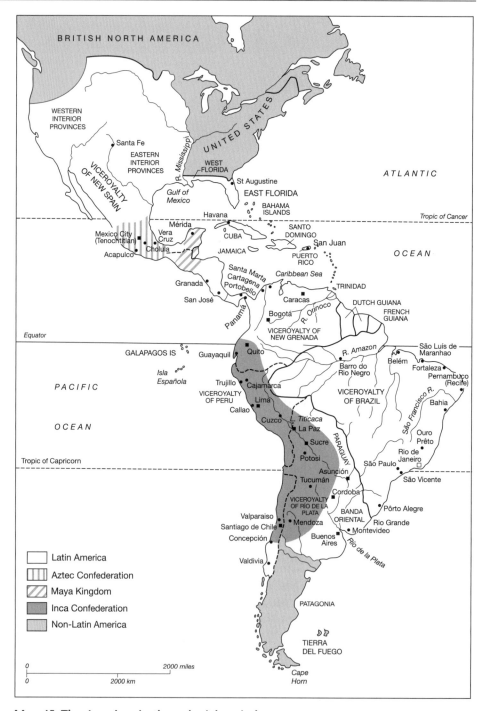

Map 45 The Americas in the colonial period
Source: After Palmer, C. (1981) *Human Cargoes*, University of Illinois Press, p. 2.

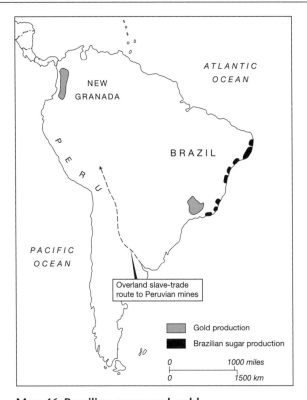

Map 46 Brazilian sugar and gold
Source: After Curtin, P. D. (1990) *The Rise and Fall of the Plantation Complex: Essays in Atlantic History, 1st Edition*, Cambridge University Press, p. 101.

acclimatization, were moved out via Cordoba to Chile, Bolivia and Peru (Map 46). This march involved severe changes in altitude and climate and proved a deadly trek for many slaves. However, the Spanish slave colonies were mainly supplied through their ports in the Caribbean, initially through ports on the isthmus of Panama and into cities along the Caribbean coastline of South America. When Spain threw open the trade in Africans (in 1789), slaves flowed into today's Colombia and Venezuela, and into the islands of Puerto Rico and Cuba (which eventually became the largest slave colony in the Spanish Americas).

Until 1738, the British sought to overcome the powerful Dutch presence in the Atlantic slave trade; by that date, the Dutch had shipped half a million Africans into the Americas. Their early trade was supplying Africans to Brazil, but after 1654, the Dutch West Indian Company turned its attention to Spanish America, under new *asiento* agreements, largely shipping Africans via the Dutch island of Curaçao. But there were also 'illegal' slave trades to Spanish colonies via the tiny Dutch island of St Eustacius. The Dutch also began to settle their own (often sickly and unstable) colonies along the river systems of the present-day Guianas: Essequibo (1618), Berbice (1627) and Suriname (1667) (Map 47). After 1795, the Dutch slave trade died away and was formally ended in 1814. Despite their importance in the early days of the Atlantic slave trade, overall the Dutch shipped only about 5 percent of the total number of Africans. From the

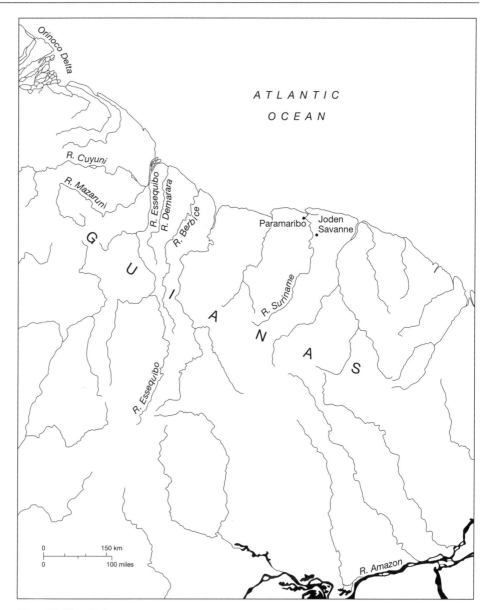

Map 47 The Guianas
Source: After Klooster, W. (1997) *The Dutch in the Americas, 1600–1800*, John Carter Brown Library, p. 62. © International Mapping.

Dutch island staging points of Curaçao and St Eustacius, Africans were trans-shipped (after the customary cleaning, feeding and recovery) to the Spanish islands, and to the Spanish ports of Portobello, Cartagena and Vera Cruz, or to the French and British islands.

For their part, the British turned to Africans in their early West Indian settlements (St Kitts, Nevis and Barbados) in the second quarter of the seventeenth century, and then, after 1655, in Jamaica (Map 48). As those islands turned to

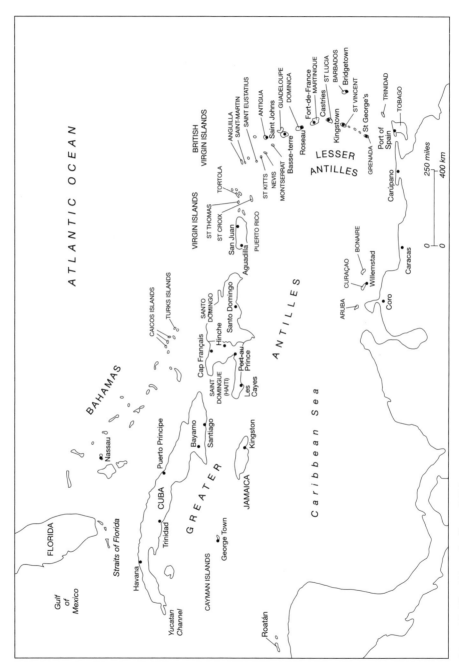

Map 48 The West Indies, 1789

Source: After Rogozinski, J. (1994) *A Brief History of the Caribbean: From the Arawak and the Carib to the Present*, Meridian Books. © 1994 by Jan Rogozinski.

sugar, so they turned to Africans. Barbados was home to 38,000 slaves in 1680, and with 1,300 new arrivals a year, the population had risen to 54,000 by 1700. By then, another 20,000 slaves toiled in the smaller British islands of St Kitts, Nevis, Antigua and Montserrat. By 1700, and with an annual importation of almost 8,000 Africans, more than a quarter of a million Africans had landed in the widely scattered islands that formed the British Caribbean.

In the British islands, the newcomers endured experiences common to slaves throughout the American settlements on landfall; of being shuffled into primitive holding quarters onshore for cleaning and feeding, sprucing up to render them fit for sale. Sometimes the slave sales took the form of a dreaded 'scramble' (where purchasers rushed in among the Africans, grabbing and securing the ones they wanted – always to the terror of the unsuspecting slave). As for the sick and the dying Africans (the 'refuse' slaves in the unforgiving vernacular of the slave traders) buyers were uninterested, leaving them to a miserable fate. Time and again, contemporaries were appalled to see human wretches discarded as 'worthless' and left to die. Many of the survivors were transshipped to other regions and islands; from Barbados to the smaller neighbouring islands, or even on to North America. Many others passed from Jamaica to Spanish America. But even those Africans who were destined for the island where they first landed had further travels ahead of them. Placed in smaller boats, they were sailed through coastal waters to remoter parts of the island, thence by foot to their final workplace.

On the eve of the French Revolution (1789), St Domingue had become *the* boom sugar colony of the Americas, its half a million slaves producing tropical produce on a scale, and at a price, that could on an open market threaten the British dominance. The importation of Africans into St Domingue *doubled* in the 1780s alone. The major point of arrival was Le Cap (Cap Français) on the island's north coast, where, as elsewhere, slaves were herded into separate quarters to be made ready for sale and onward movement to that huge island's sugar plantations, or to the coffee plantations at higher elevation. So great was the flow of Africans into St Domingue in the second half of the eighteenth century that the baracoons were regularly filled with Africans awaiting sale and dispatch to a final destination.

The French, like other European maritime and colonial powers, had long been keen to establish their own slave settlements in the Americas and had secured a string of West Indian islands, notably St Kitts, Guadeloupe and Martinique. As those islands turned to sugar, so their populations became African. By 1700, some 155,000 had landed in the French West Indies, but after 1713 (the Treaty of Utrecht), French ships transported one million Africans to the French West Indies. The French sugar revolution took place initially on Martinique, Guadeloupe and St Christopher (St Kitts), but it was the subsequent development of sugar (later coffee) on St Domingue that prompted the dramatic rise to dominance of the French slave/sugar system. By the mid-eighteenth century, St Domingue had the largest slave population in the Caribbean. In 1789, the island's slave population of 460,000 was almost half of the total one million slaves in the entire Caribbean (Klein, 32–3). St Domingue was a massive, mountainous island, and the newly arrived Africans' workplaces were generally far away from their arrival point on the island; more sailing or trekking was needed to reach the place where the Africans were put to a lifetime's work. Here as elsewhere, arrival did not mean the end of wearying travels for the Africans.

Many Africans destined for North America had stopped initially in the West Indies, but the development of tobacco in the Chesapeake and rice in South Carolina saw a growing proportion of Africans landed direct from Africa. The Chesapeake region lacked one central port, and slaves were sold at various points up and down that complex riverine system. North American merchants bought groups of Africans, marching them to more distant points where they were sold again, in small batches or individually, to local slave owners. Consequently, slave ships entering the Chesapeake took as long as two months to complete the sale of their human cargoes. It was different in Carolina, where slaves were sold in larger groups and were sometimes imported to order.

The first Africans in North America had arrived in Virginia; by the early years of the eighteenth century perhaps 7,700 had arrived. Africans began to arrive in Charleston in numbers at the beginning of the eighteenth century, and South Carolina continued to import growing numbers of Africans up to and beyond American independence to fuel the rice economy. Africans arriving in Charleston were put up for sale within two weeks of arrival (after quarantine had been cleared on Sullivan's Island off the Charleston coast) and generally found themselves put to work on their new plantation homes within a month. Often sold as one lot from the Charleston slave auction, Africans were competed for by crowds of planters, who, keen to augment their labour force, had converged on the city from great distances.

These two colonies (Virginia and South Carolina) were distinguished by the critical fact that, from the 1720s, the slave population of Virginia began to reproduce itself; it no longer required large imports of Africans. However, South Carolina continued to rely on Africans right up to the ending of the slave trade in 1807. And there, as in the West Indies, the more Africans (i.e. largely male) there were in the population, the more difficult it was for the slave population to grow naturally (Map 49).

The other, initially minor, arrival point for Africans into North America was Louisiana (Spanish, then French, before becoming part of the USA in 1803). Between its effective foundation in 1719 and 1743, French ships landed almost 6,000 Africans in Louisiana. By 1740, the slave population of that settlement stood at almost 4,000; perhaps 5,600 by 1770, growing to 18,700 in 1790 before almost doubling by 1810.

The abolition of the Atlantic slave trade by the British and the Americans in 1807 did *not* stop the flow of Africans across the Atlantic. Despite diplomatic and naval pressure, slave traders were able to ship more than three million Africans into the Americas, mainly to Brazil, Cuba and Puerto Rico, with smaller numbers to Spanish America and the French islands. Africans were deposited at a number of disembarkation points, from Santos to Havana. Again, they were all subject to onward travel to their final workplace, redistributed to new slave-based economies in the Brazilian, Cuban or Puerto Rican interior.

The ten+ million African survivors of the Atlantic crossing were landed at a huge number of destinations. All had travelled vast distances, on land and

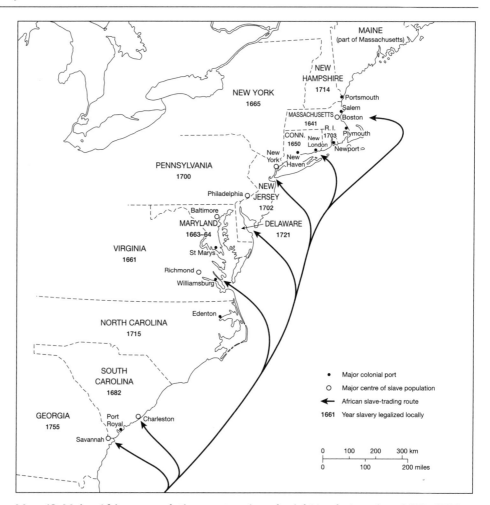

Map 49 Major African population centres in colonial North America, 1633–1755
Source: Copyright © 2000. From *The Routledge Atlas of African American History* by J. Earle.
Reproduced by permission of Routledge/Taylor & Francis Books, Inc.

water. Though the Middle Passage was the most horrific of experiences, it was preceded and followed by other journeys, sometimes of the most distressing kind. Africans fanned out, from the very edges of North American settlement in the Piedmont to the high-altitude settlements in Central and South America, and to the newly settled lands of the Caribbean islands and mainland Americas. In time, their descendants were to help to populate all corners of the Americas – and even beyond.

CHAPTER 13

Brazil

The story of slavery in the Americas effectively begins and ends in Brazil even though slaves were introduced to Hispaniola and Cuba earlier. Slavery first took root in Brazil in the late sixteenth century, and Brazil was the last country in the Americas to abolish slavery – in 1888. In the intervening period, more than four million Africans arrived in the slave ships.

The initial Portuguese interest in Brazil in the early sixteenth century was in barter and trade. Native Indians and Portuguese traded imported goods for timber, but this quickly gave way to permanent Portuguese settlement via royal land grants. The development of sugar plantations – or *engenhos* – in the north-east (notably Pernambuco) led to dramatic change in relations with the local Indians. From the first, Brazilian sugar faced labour problems. Local Indians were resistant to the demanding labour regime of sugar, and the Portuguese settlers began to enslave Indians for the plantations (and for other agricultural labour). It was a trend that was resisted by local Jesuits. As sugar expanded (there were sixty sugar mills in operation by the 1570s) the demand for labour increased, and Portugal turned to Africans as slaves, a move that seemed both natural and logical, not least because the Portuguese *already* used African slaves both in Portugal itself and in the Atlantic islands. Brazil began to import slaves direct from Portuguese trading posts on the African coast, especially from Angola, which rapidly established itself as the most important source of labour for the development of Brazilian slavery. In the process, a South Atlantic slave trade (and wider trade route) was created that survived through to the nineteenth century (Maps 50 and 51).

Sugar drove forward the development of Brazilian slavery, and as the colonial settlement of Brazil advanced, edging away from the pioneering coastal regions, each new development turned to slaves for its labouring task force. Slavery was no longer uniquely associated with sugar but spilled into newly developed re-gions from its initial base in the sugar economy. It spread for example to Minas Gerais (gold) in the early eighteenth century, later into the agricultural planta-tions of Amazonia. The end result was that Brazil imported huge numbers of Africans. Some 20,000 Africans a year were shipped to Brazil in the eighteenth century, rising still further in the 1820s and 1830s with the opening of mining regions. The country bucked the abolitionist trend of the nineteenth century: just when the zealous British had embarked on global abolition, Brazil demanded ever more Africans for labour in its expansive frontier society. Despite British diplomatic pressure, despite the persistent abolitionist presence in the Atlantic of the Royal Navy, some one million Africans were shipped to Brazil in the nineteenth century before Brazilian emancipation in 1888. Much of Brazil's

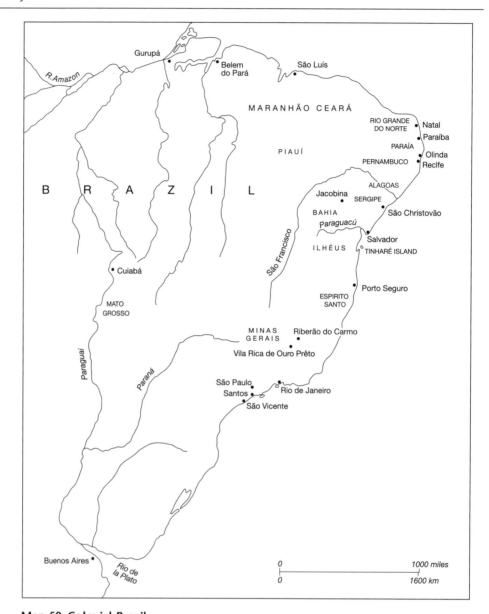

Map 50 Colonial Brazil

Source: After Schwartz, S. B. (1985) *Sugar Plantations in the Formation of Brazilian Society: Bahia, 1550–1835*, Cambridge University Press, p. 21.

continuing demand for slaves was a result of its economic and geographical expansion, but, like the West Indies in the previous century, the slaves already resident in Brazil had unusually low levels of reproduction (exacerbated by the preponderance of male slaves). The end result was that Brazilian slavery, with its regular infusions of new arrivals, was very *African* until the mid-nineteenth century. This had major cultural consequences for the development of Brazilian society: Brazil was, and remained long after emancipation, a very African society (Maps 52–54).

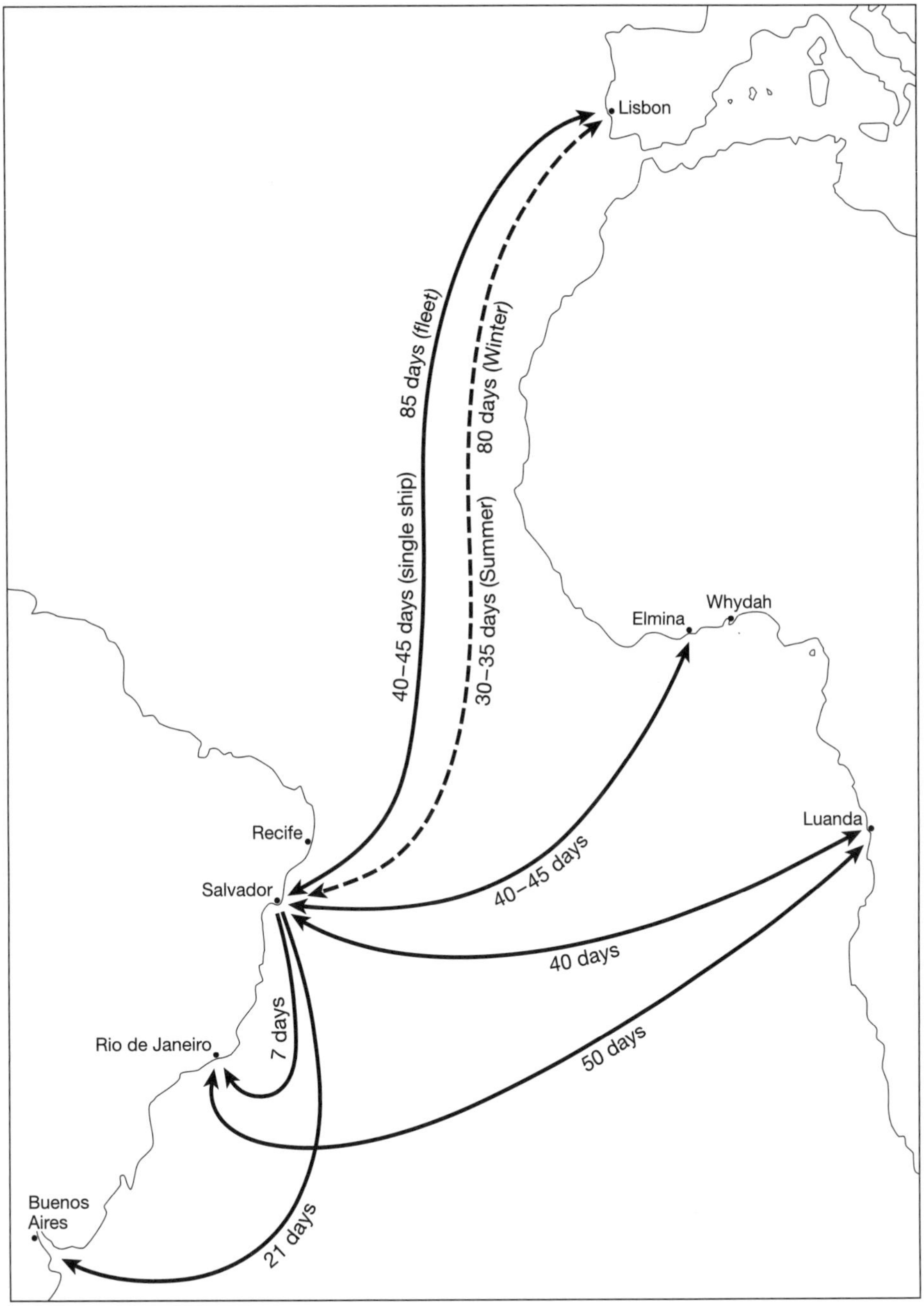

Map 51 Approximate sailing times to/from Brazil in the seventeenth and eighteenth centuries

Source: After Schwartz, S. B. (1985) *Sugar Plantations in the Formation of Brazilian Society: Bahia, 1550–1835*, Cambridge University Press, p. 182.

Map 52 Nineteenth-century Brazil

Source: After Curtin, P. D. (1990) *The Rise and Fall of the Plantation Complex: Essays in Atlantic History, 1st Edition*, Cambridge University Press, p. 194.

Though sugar had been the initial inspiration for Brazilian slavery, slavery had quickly spilled into all corners of Brazilian life and economy. Slaves, of course, dominated all aspects of sugar cultivation and production, but they also worked in cattle, tobacco, cotton and coffee production. They worked in gold mines, and were seen throughout Brazilian towns, mainly as domestic workers and casual labouring gangs. Brazil was also a slave-owning society like no other in the Americas. Even the humblest of free people acquired slaves for their economic activity or their homes. Black slavery dominated Brazil's human landscape, in town and country. All Brazil's major cities inevitably had large slave communities, again unlike other slave societies in the Americas. Equally, a marked proportion of slaves were freed and Brazil quickly became home to the largest community of free blacks (and people of colour) anywhere in the Americas.

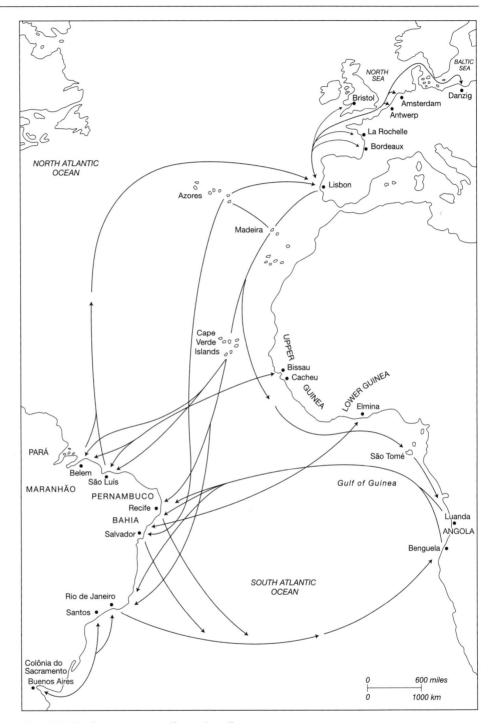

Map 53 Trading routes to/from Brazil

Source: After Russell-Wood, A. J. R. (1998) *The Portuguese Empire, 1415–1808: A World on the Move*, The Johns Hopkins University Press, p. 139. Copyright © 1992, 1998 A. J. R. Russell-Wood.

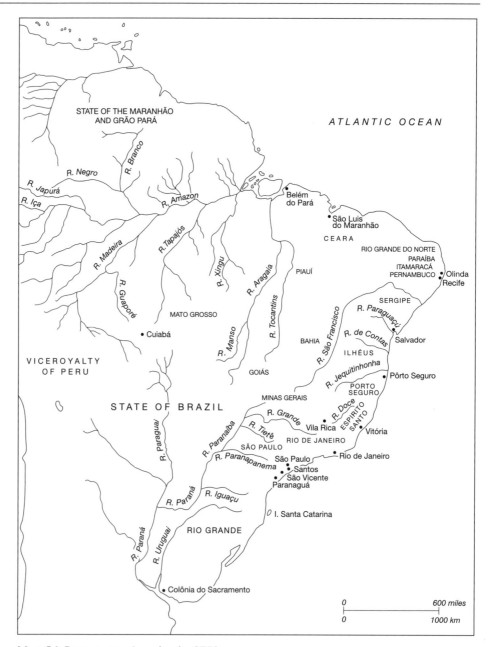

Map 54 Portuguese America in 1750

Source: After Russell-Wood, A. J. R. (1998) *The Portuguese Empire, 1415–1808: A World on the Move*, The Johns Hopkins University Press. Copyright © 1992, 1998 A. J. R. Russell-Wood.

At every level, Brazil was exceptional. For instance, at the very time that the British slave system was under attack, Brazilian slavery continued to thrive.

Even so, Brazil could not remain immune from the global encroachment of abolitionist ideas, and Brazilian slave owners found themselves increasingly on the defensive in the early nineteenth century. The first defeat for Brazilian slavery was the abolition of the Brazilian slave trade, effectively in 1850. By then, too, global opinion (and powerful groups within Brazil) had come to see slavery as an archaic reminder of the past. After 1871, when all children born to slave mothers were freed, the end of Brazilian slavery was clearly in sight. Gradually it withered, amid a spluttering, divided defence and a radical opposition. By the time it was finally abolished in 1888, only 5 percent of the Brazilian population were slaves.

Brazil gave birth to slavery in the Americas, and Brazil clung to slavery longer than any other country in the hemisphere. Its consequence for the nature and development of Brazil was enormous. The impact on Africa was almost incalculable.

CHAPTER 14

The Caribbean

The European invasion and settlement of the Americas was in large measure determined at first by geography. In the Caribbean, the Europeans faced a complexity of physical geography, from virtually inaccessible mountain ranges and peaks to remarkably fertile valleys and coastlines, through to tiny arid islands, and others that are little more than the unusable tips of submerged mountains. And all this along an island arc that stretches 4,000 kilometres from Cuba to Trinidad. It forms a region that is amazingly varied: subject to earthquakes, volcanoes and annual threats from hurricanes. At the time of Columbus's arrival, many of the islands were covered by rain forests, but that, along with much of the natural flora and fauna, has been removed by man over the past five centuries. Much the same happened to the indigenous people, the Taino Indians, whose different sub-groups were scattered across the islands and whose history we are only now beginning to reconstruct. Their numbers are uncertain, but they were greatly reduced by the arrival of the Europeans, by violence, by the introduction of European diseases, by white domination, and by the new demands for work placed on them by Europeans.

After their first tentative settlements in the Caribbean, the Spanish began to use a number of strategically located islands as invaluable way stations between Spain and the wealth of their empire in Central and South America. The islands provided natural stopping-off points for travel to and from Central America: Santo Domingo in Hispaniola on the westerly route from Spain into the Caribbean, and Havana in Cuba, back home from Central America and out into the Atlantic through the Straits of Florida. The Spaniards assembled their convoys and treasure ships at secure anchorages, on the isthmus and islands, before heading across the Atlantic. However, this proved an irresistible attraction for privateers from northern Europe, who began to prey on those fleets. Despite the wealth involved, despite the destruction and friction inevitably caused, this phase – of the islands being largely stepping stones – was temporary. In time, the islands began to yield an even greater bounty to successful (and lucky) European settlers. With the assistance of Dutch money and practical experience of settlement and trade both in the Atlantic and Brazil, French and English settlers began to put down roots in the Caribbean, first in St Kitts and Barbados. Survival was the first aim, thereafter their goal was to produce commercial export crops. As land was cleared, a mix of settlers, indentured white labourers and a handful of African slaves experimented with a variety of crops. They tried tobacco and cotton and other minor crops. With the encouragement of the government and backers in England, settlers moved on to neighbouring islands: Nevis (1628), Antigua and Montserrat (1632). On some islands, settlers were initially driven off by Indians. At the same time, the French laid claim to their own islands, notably Martinique. They too were kept out of other islands by fierce Indian (Carib) resistance. The successful settlements were greatly helped by imported goods and foodstuffs from the colonies in North America. From the early days of the English Caribbean settlements, critical economic and social links were forged with North America. It was also one of the critical strands in the broader structure of an unfolding Atlantic economy (Maps 55 and 56).

As with Brazil earlier, the coming of sugar transformed everything. Tried earlier by Spanish settlers on their islands (Jamaica and Hispaniola), sugar took hold in Barbados and St Kitts, thanks to Dutch sugar expertise from Brazil. English planters were quick to grasp the need for economies of scale: sugar was grown more profitably on larger plantations. As more and more (and bigger) plantations blossomed across the islands, the landscape of Barbados itself changed. So too did the population. Labour was initially recruited from indentured white immigrants and from prisoners transported during the English Civil War. But as sugar boomed, planters turned to African labour.

For their part, once freed from their indentures, many local whites moved elsewhere (to Jamaica, to North America and South America). In their place, Africans began to arrive in Barbados in their thousands. There were perhaps 20,000 slaves in Barbados in 1653; by 1666, that had grown to 33,184. By then, black had begun to outnumber white. The natural wilderness gave way to man-made and orderly agricultural systems – increasingly to plantations. Similarly, the local people had changed. Indigenous peoples made way for a changing mosaic of black and white, free and unfree and indentured. Their efforts concentrated on the production of export crops to England and to Europe. There, tropical produce had begun to transform the habits and the diet of Europeans. The speed of the physical and commercial transformation of Barbados took everyone by surprise, especially following the introduction of sugar. Barbados pointed the way for other Caribbean islands. Settlers on some of the smaller islands had tried to emulate the pattern, but it was the English settlement of Jamaica in 1655 that relocated the centre of the English Caribbean sugar industry.

In Jamaica, soldiers from Cromwell's invading force, his 'Western Design' (recruited largely from other islands, along with other regional migrants), formed the core of the new settler class, fanning out on to the fertile land granted to them from the crown after 1660. After initial efforts at cultivating various crops, they turned to sugar. The Jamaican sugar industry took off in the last twenty-five years of the seventeenth century, overtaking Barbados in the early eighteenth century. By 1775, Jamaica produced half of Britain's sugar. By then, sugar cultivation had spread throughout all the British – and French – islands (Maps 57–59).

Despite international war, Indian attacks, slave insurrections and natural disasters, the sugar islands thrived, none more spectacularly than Jamaica. The largest of the British islands, Jamaica seemed to offer plenty of land to the adventurous planter and his slave gangs, but nothing was possible without the Africans. Geography was against the Jamaican planters, for they were at the end of a long maritime leg across the island chain for ships from Africa that had first made landfall in Barbados or the Leewards. Nonetheless, the slave population

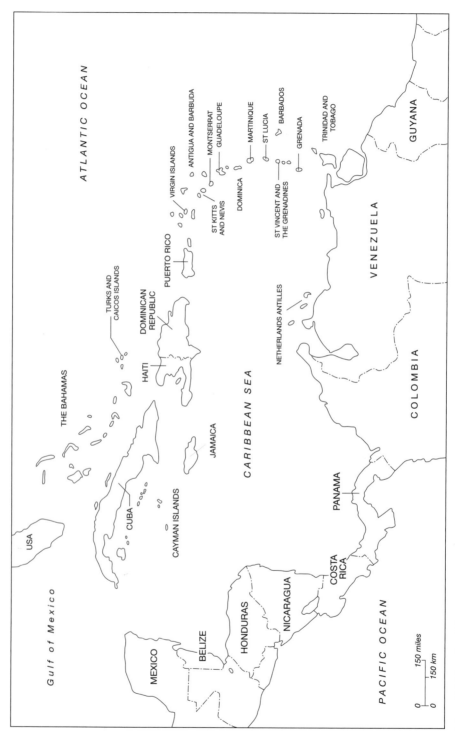

Map 55 The Caribbean

Source: After Rogozinski, J. (1994) *A Brief History of the Caribbean: From the Arawak and the Carib to the Present*, Meridian Books, p. 294. © 1994 by Jan Rogozinski.

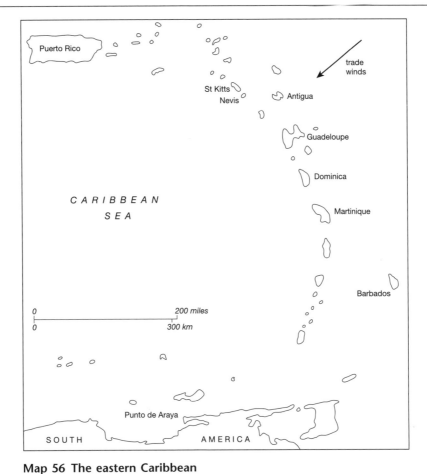

Map 56 The eastern Caribbean
Source: After Curtin, P. D. (1990) *The Rise and Fall of the Plantation Complex: Essays in Atlantic History, 1st Edition*, Cambridge University Press, p. 74.

doubled in the thirty years to 1730, though Jamaican planters still wanted more. So too did planters throughout the Caribbean. In 1655, there were about 50,000 blacks in the West Indies, slightly less than the white population. But at the time of emancipation (1833), that had increased to 1,109,561 blacks, compared with 659,588 whites. Everywhere, the black population grew.

The British acquired new West Indian islands throughout the eighteenth century, via war and peace treaties, and settlers from older islands migrated to new prospects in St Vincent, Dominica, Grenada and Tobago. Everywhere they created new sugar plantations. A similar pattern unfolded (though more slowly at first) in the French islands. The most spectacular development took place in St Domingue. By the late 1760s, that colony produced as much sugar cane as the whole of the British West Indies. Both Martinique and Guadeloupe also expanded their sugar production, but not on the scale or at the pace of St Domingue. It seemed that Europeans – the market for Caribbean sugar – simply could not get enough sugar. After 1763, Cuba also turned to sugar cultivation in a major way, prompted by British help and slave traders who imported

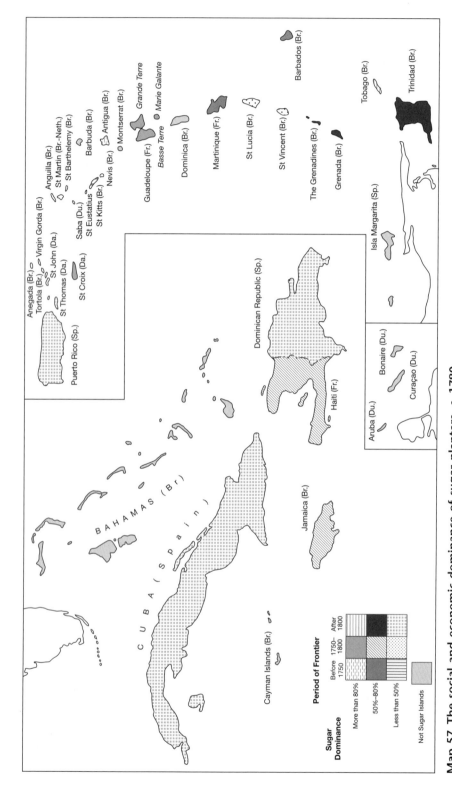

Map 57 The social and economic dominance of sugar planters, c. 1780

Source: Stinchcombe, Arthur L.; *Sugar Island Slavery in the Age of Enlightenment.* © 1995 Princeton University Press. Reprinted by permission of Princeton University Press.

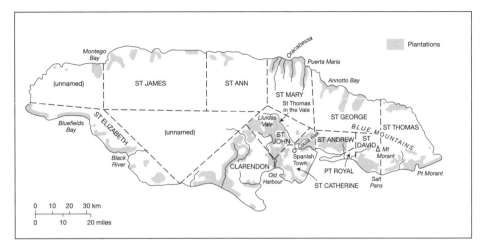

Map 58 The proliferation of plantations in Jamaica, c. 1670
Source: After 1774 map by Edward Long, in Watts, D. (1987) *The West Indies: Patterns of Development, Culture and Environmental Change since 1492*, Cambridge University Press, Figure 7.2.

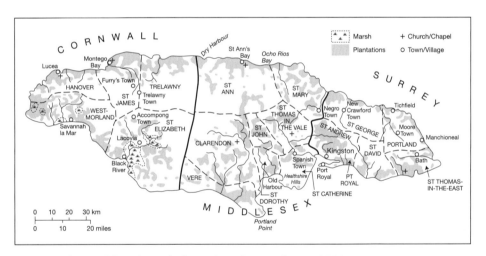

Map 59 The proliferation of plantations in Jamaica, c. 1774
Source: After 1774 map by Edward Long, in Watts, D. (1987) *The West Indies: Patterns of Development, Culture and Environmental Change since 1492*, Cambridge University Press, Figure 7.2.

10,000 slaves to push forward the Cuban sugar revolution. Sugar poured across the Atlantic to Europe. The British imported 8,176 tons in 1663, 25,000 tons in 1710 and more than 97,000 tons in 1775, most consumed in Britain. By the 1770s, the British were consuming eleven pounds of sugar per head annually. Sugar and rum transformed British eating and drinking habits, creating the national addiction for sweetness that has characterized the British diet from that day to this.

Everywhere the key was the African. Europeans all agreed that Africans, later their locally born descendants, were essential to the task of converting fertile Caribbean lands to profitable cultivation. Thus, from one island to another, armies of Africans were imported, acclimatized and then settled on to the sugar plantations. The process was most striking on the bigger islands: Jamaica, Cuba, St Domingue and Puerto Rico. The West Indian population became ever more African. By 1750, about 800,000 Africans had been imported into the region, though by then the actual slave population stood at only 300,000. There was a discrepancy throughout the islands between the numbers imported and the numbers in the population, but the explanation was simple. The sugar islands were a 'graveyard for slaves'. And the more the planters bought, the more they had to buy to fill the ranks of those who had died (normally of ailments imported from Africa and the slave ships). All the human data we possess (mortality, birth rates, levels of sickness) were at their worst among African slaves. And these data were worst of all among sugar slaves. Yet sugar dominated the lives of ever more slaves on the islands in the eighteenth century. Sugar was king to the extent that by the late eighteenth century 60 percent of slaves worked in sugar in the British islands. On the smaller islands, one slave in ten worked in sugar.

However, this concentration on sugar can deceive. Slaves worked in most corners of the islands' economies: as domestics, as urban workers, as traders and hawkers, as independent cultivators, as skilled artisans, as cattlemen and drivers. They worked on coffee plantations at higher altitude, especially in the booming coffee industry of St Domingue, they laboured on the docks and quaysides, and on board ocean-going vessels and on boats in inland waters. And much of this was also true of slave women, both young and old, though certain jobs were allocated by sex and age.

The consequences of this growing reliance on slaves on all the West Indian islands and in all corners of the economy was a staggering rise in imports of Africans to the Caribbean. The peoples and cultures of the islands, though transformed by adaptation to life in the islands and to the relationships with Europeans, struck outsiders as an image of Africa. Yet here, surely, is a remarkable curiosity. Millions of Africans had been shipped thousands of miles, in unimaginable conditions, to produce tropical produce for Western taste. Yet the people who consumed those goods (first the Europeans and settlers in the Americas, later the people of the wider world) had previously managed to survive *without* such produce. Slavery had been instrumental in stimulating, then satisfying, some of the critical social habits of the wider world. Few of those involved doubted that here was a profitable system (except of course for the slaves). At its most obvious in the Caribbean and Brazil (and almost 90 percent of all Africans were landed in those two regions), African slavery had come to dominate tropical agriculture. But it had also slipped into most corners of colonial America, and had even touched Europe itself.

CHAPTER 15

North America

African slaves were imported into North America much as they were elsewhere in the Americas. The guiding force behind North American slavery was primarily British and to a lesser extent French and Spanish (in the Gulf region). Those North American communities that turned to the plantation mode of production – for tobacco and rice, later for cotton – turned inevitably to black enslaved labour. In the colonies of the 'Old South', slavery was integral to local economic

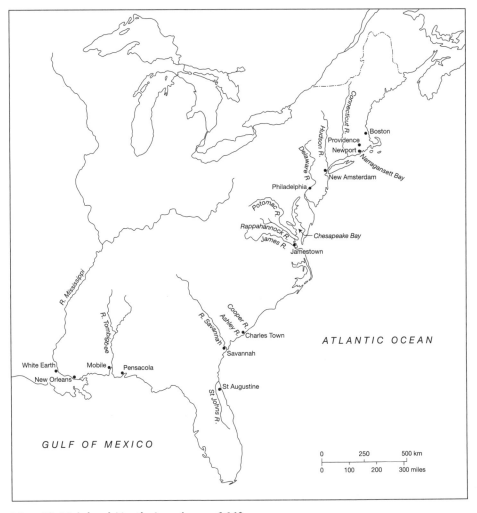

Map 60 Mainland North America, c. 1660

Map 61 Mainland North America, c. 1790

development, though black slaves never outnumbered whites as they did in the Caribbean or Brazil. Moreover, North American slavery was different from the slave systems that emerged in Brazil and the Caribbean. There was a basic demographic difference (Maps 60 and 61).

Until the 1720s, the black population of North America grew via imported Africans. Thereafter, it began to increase naturally rather than via the Atlantic slave trade. The consequences of the diminishing importance of the Atlantic slave trade on North America were enormous. Africa and its multitude of cultures receded as a demographic force in the lives of local slaves: there were fewer and fewer Africans in slave communities. This had the effect of inevitably reducing the cultural influence of Africa, though there were notable exceptions, in South Carolina's Sea Islands for example. But we need to ask a simple question. What were Africans doing in North America in the first place?

Though the first Africans landed in Jamestown in 1619, slavery did not take root until the conversion of the Chesapeake region to tobacco cultivation. Even

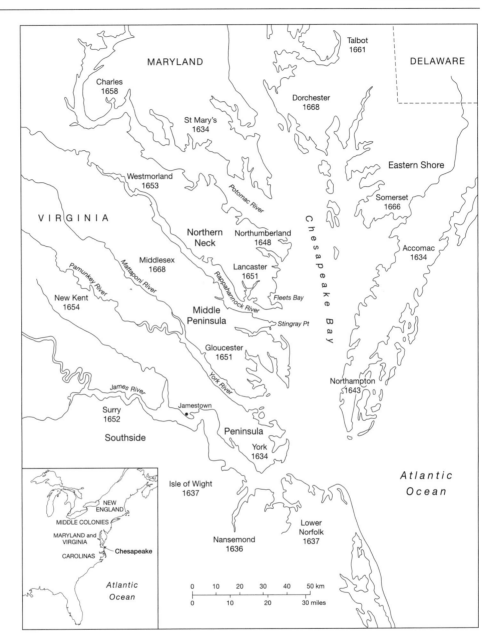

Map 62 The Chesapeake in the seventeenth century

Source: After Canny, N. (ed.) (1998) *The Oxford History of the British Empire: Volume I: The Origins of Empire: British Overseas Enterprise to the Close of the Seventeenth Century*, Map 8.1, p. 172. By permission of Oxford University Press.

then, slavery was slow to take off because the early tobacco industry used indentured white labour. Slavery developed because indentured whites expected both their freedom and land at the end of their indenture. African slaves had no such expectations. By the 1690s, 3,500 Africans had been imported into Virginia to service the expanding tobacco industry (Maps 62–63). By comparison, the West Indian colonies at that time were dominated by slaves. In the 1720s, African

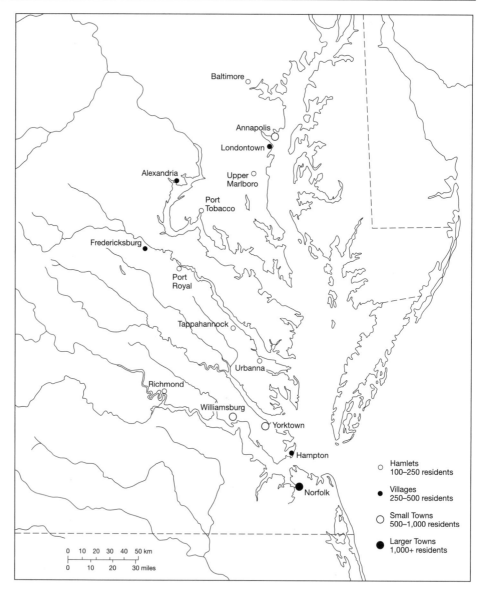

Map 63 Town development on the tobacco coast of the Chesapeake, c. 1750
Source: From *Tobacco and Slaves: The Development of Southern Cultures in the Chesapeake, 1680–1800*
by Allan Kulikoff. Copyright © 1986 by the University of North Carolina Press. Used by permission
of the publisher.

imports into Virginia had risen to 15,000. Thereafter, however, the natural
increase of the local slave population saw a decline in the import of Africans. It
was different further south, where Africans continued to flood into South Carolina (and into Georgia from the 1750s). Some 60,000 slaves lived in the lower
South (the Carolinas and Georgia) by the mid-eighteenth century. By then,
slaves comprised 20 percent of the total population of British North America,
though they were heavily concentrated in Maryland, Virginia, the Carolinas and
the newly founded Georgia (Map 64).

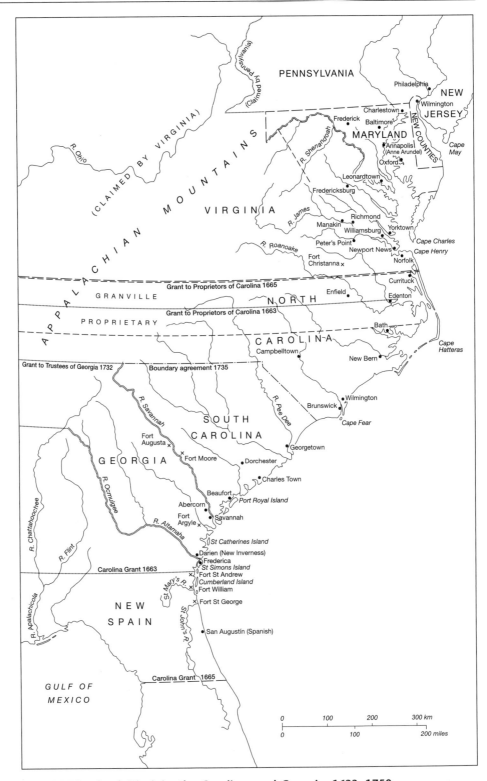

Map 64 Maryland, Virginia, the Carolinas and Georgia, 1633–1750

Source: After *The American Heritage Pictorial Atlas of US History* (1966), American Heritage Publishing Company, p. 49.

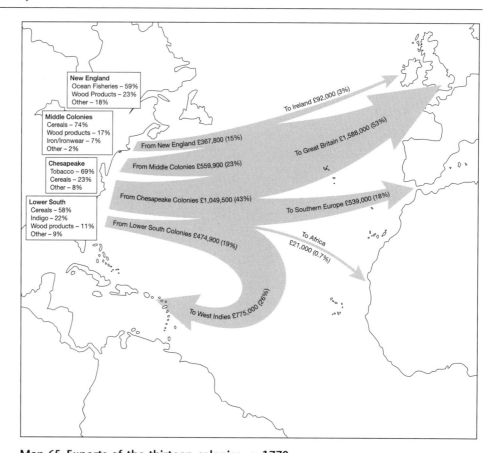

Map 65 Exports of the thirteen colonies, c. 1770

Source: From *Encyclopedia of the North American Colonies*, 3V, edited by J. E. Cooke, © 1994, Charles Scribner's Sons. Reprinted by permission of The Gale Group.

It seems hardly worth saying that slavery was a harsh institution, shaped by punitive local colonial laws and administered on the ground by violence and retribution. It had its critics (voices that spoke up for the slaves and denounced the miseries of their lives), but they, like others elsewhere, were generally disregarded in the rush to make money from slave-based activities. Humanity and concern for the slaves were swept aside by the power of commerce.

By the mid-eighteenth century, huge volumes of slave-grown produce were being shipped across the Atlantic to Britain (Maps 65–67). In 1750, for example, tobacco accounted for half of all exports from British North America, some £70 million. The expansion of rice production was equally dramatic. Between 1710 and 1750, rice exports from South Carolina increased from £1.5 million to £27 million (Map 68). By then, that region was also exporting substantial volumes of indigo (for dye). Indeed, South Carolina had now outstripped the Chesapeake planters in the value of their exports; but all came courtesy of their slaves' efforts.

In the North American colonies, as in the Caribbean, slaves quickly moved into all corners of local social and economic life. Though slaves dominated certain industries and regions, they could be found everywhere. There were for example sizeable *urban* black populations, and slaves could be counted among

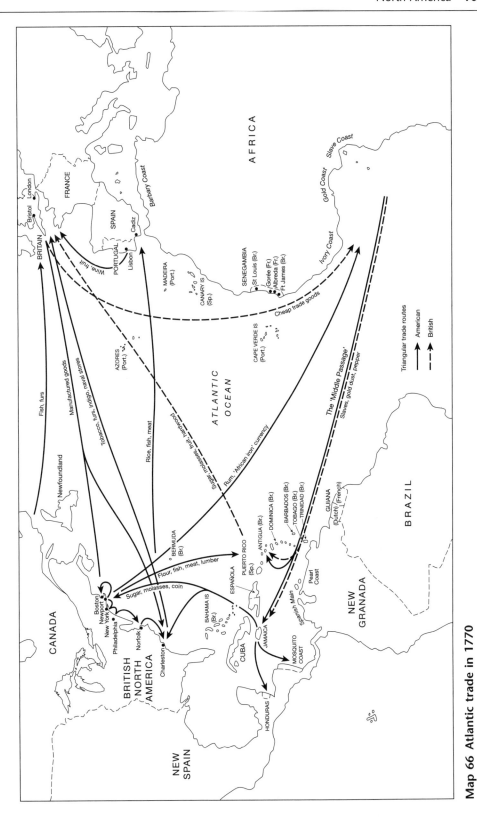

Map 66 Atlantic trade in 1770

Source: After Ferrell, R. H. and Natkiel, R. (1993) *Atlas of American History, 3rd Edition*, Facts on File, Inc. © 1993 by Richard Natkiel.

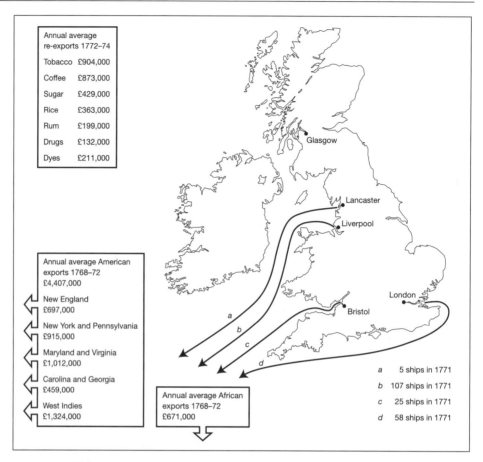

Annual average
re-exports 1772–74

Tobacco	£904,000
Coffee	£873,000
Sugar	£429,000
Rice	£363,000
Rum	£199,000
Drugs	£132,000
Dyes	£211,000

Glasgow

Lancaster

Liverpool

London

Annual average American
exports 1768–72
£4,407,000

New England
£697,000

New York and Pennsylvania
£915,000

Maryland and Virginia
£1,012,000

Carolina and Georgia
£459,000

West Indies
£1,324,000

Bristol

Annual average African
exports 1768–72
£671,000

a	5 ships in 1771
b	107 ships in 1771
c	25 ships in 1771
d	58 ships in 1771

Map 67 British exports to the Atlantic area and re-exports of Atlantic commodities: annual averages
Source: After Porter, A. (ed.) (1991) *Atlas of British Overseas Expansion*, Routledge, p. 47.

skilled workers in all walks of life, from metalwork through to navigating the waterways of the Chesapeake and the river systems of South Carolina. Slaves cared for their owners' every domestic need, looked after (and helped to rear) their children, and catered for the most intimate of domestic needs and habits. Slaves were in fact ubiquitous, from market stalls and corner hawkers in local towns, and the dockside, to the quiet recesses of white domesticity.

There were major differences between the two slave systems of colonial North America (tobacco and rice). The climate and topography were different; tobacco slaves worked on relatively small plantations and were owned, on the whole, in small groups, working to a distinct tobacco system of agriculture. This was quite unlike the task system that evolved in rice cultivation, in which the geography and work regime were much harsher and more unpleasant. It was more like sugar cultivation in the Caribbean in its physical unpleasantness and in its consequences for the slaves.

Blacks could also be found outside these two dominant regions. By 1750, there were 11,000 in New England and 21,000 in Delaware, New Jersey, New York and Pennsylvania, but slavery never had the economic importance in the North that

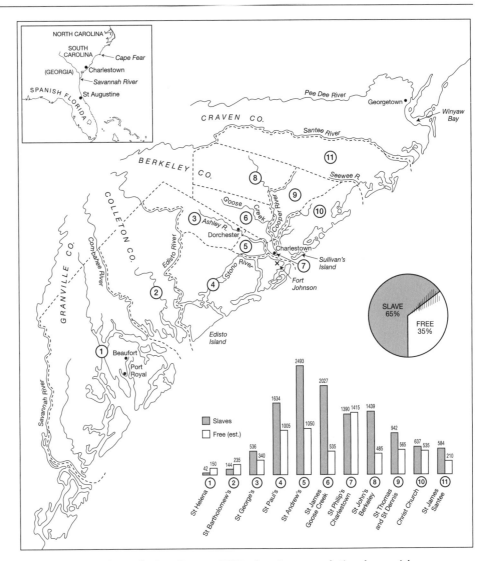

Map 68 Colonial South Carolina, c. 1720, showing population by parishes
Source: From *Black Majority* by Peter H. Wood, copyright © 1974 by Peter H. Wood. Used by permission of Alfred A. Knopf, a division of Random House, Inc.

it acquired in the South. When the American colonies broke away from Britain in 1776, they took with them half a million blacks; by 1810, that had increased to 1.4 million, over-welmingly in the Old South. It was this *established* American slave population that was to make possible the development of the enslaved cotton revolution of the nineteenth century and the consequent westward movement of slavery from the former colonies to the new cotton frontier. When cotton thrived in the new states of the South and the frontier in the nineteenth century, the new cotton plantations turned for their labour not to Africa but to the slave populations of the old slave systems on the east coast (see Map 49). In the process, slavery was thus transformed from a British colonial institution into a critical element in the early growth and expansion of the infant republic. The slavery of British colonial North America gave birth to slavery in the USA.

CHAPTER 16

Cotton and the USA

The association between cotton and slavery is embedded deep in US history and folk memory. The concept and popular images of 'the South' are so entangled with cotton – and slavery – that they tend to be linked automatically: cotton *means* slavery. But as with other slave-grown produce, the story of cotton has an unusual historical trajectory. Cotton had been grown in various New World settlements long before Sea Island cotton was transplanted from the Bahamas to mainland America during the American Revolution. However, it was the short-staple variety of cotton that became the basis of the American cotton revolution. This followed the introduction of Eli Whitney's cotton gin after 1793, allowing cultivation in upland and inland locations, shifting cotton away from its old coastal locations. By 1800, this type of cotton had begun to replace tobacco in up-country Georgia. There, it was grown by slave labour, the slaves having migrated with white settlers moving from the old slave regions of Virginia and South Carolina. The indigenous people were moved out, and slaves were moved in, along what became an internal US slave-trading route. Slaves from the old slave-owning east began cultivation of cotton in newly settled frontier regions.

Whitney's cotton gin made possible the development of huge tracts in the lower South. Though cotton was less successful in some areas of the South, by 1850 the region was producing almost 2.5 million bales of cotton per year, each of 400 lb. That figure had doubled ten years later. It was, once again, made possible by the expansion of slavery and of slave holding. On the eve of the Civil War, there were no fewer than 400,000 slave owners (most of whom owned only a handful of slaves). By the mid-century, there were almost four million slaves, though only about 60 percent worked in cotton (Map 69). The USA no longer needed to import slaves from Africa, the slave states relying instead on an *internal* slave trade. American slave traders acquired slaves from the old slave states, and moved them by foot and by water, east and south to the expanding cotton frontier. Others simply accompanied their migrating owners as they resettled in the new cotton regions (Map 70). As cotton expanded, slavery became ever more deeply embedded in American life, even though increases in slave prices sometimes threatened the economic viability of slavery. Through it all, through panics and market blips, the slave-owning South clung ever more doggedly to the slave system. By mid-century, slave owning in the USA had become a way of life, a distinct culture to which slave owners adhered tenaciously, especially in the face of mounting criticism of slavery from the North and overseas.

The development of cotton in the South saw the emergence of a new trading axis. With the growth of cotton plantations in Alabama, Louisiana and Mississippi, trade flowed in and out of Mobile and New Orleans, thence across the Atlantic to Liverpool and on to the cotton factories of Lancashire. Slaves had settled in

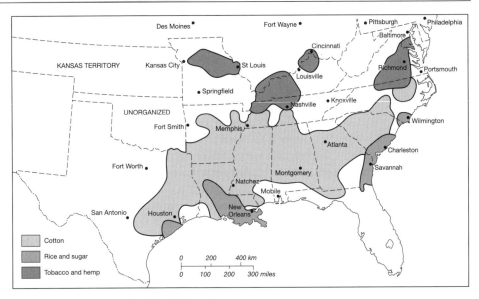

Map 69 Major crops in the US South

Source: Adapted from *The American Heritage Pictorial Atlas of US History* (1966), American Heritage Publishing Company, p. 189.

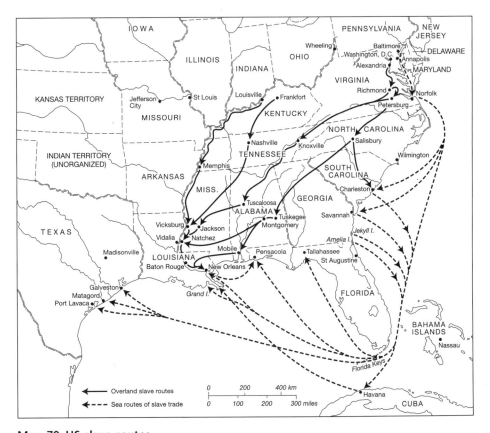

Map 70 US slave routes

Source: Adapted from *The American Heritage Pictorial Atlas of US History* (1966), American Heritage Publishing Company.

Louisiana from the early days of French and Spanish settlement, having been imported direct from Africa, and they formed roughly half of the colony's population of 32,062 in 1785. They were augmented after the Haitian revolution of 1791, when French refugees and their slaves fled to Louisiana. These emigré French planters developed a thriving sugar industry in southern Louisiana in the 1790s, but the real transformation in Louisiana was affected by the coming of cotton and the growth of New Orleans as the *entrepôt* for the Mississippi valley. Though New Orleans developed its own distinct urban slave culture, with social ramifications down to the present day, the real value of slaves was to be found in the cotton hinterland of the Gulf coast.

It was cotton that powered the rise of Louisiana and the Gulf coast, but it was in New Orleans and Mobile that some of the most enduring images of slavery developed: the infamous slave sales of the late slave period, with slaves imported from the east being sold on the auction blocks for hundreds, sometimes thousands of dollars. This was the process of being sold 'down the river' (the Mississippi) to New Orleans to work in nearby sugar-producing parishes (with their reliance primarily on male slaves) or in the cotton fields of the American interior.

In the fifty years before the Civil War, the slave population of the South exploded. Louisiana increased from 34,660 to more than a third of a million. Most slaves were owned by a very small number of planters: most lived and worked in heavy concentrations of slaves on the richest of soils, close to the sustaining rivers. Louisiana's slaves were the most productive in the nation. The wealth they generated enriched the dominant owners and traders, helped to convert local towns into cities of considerable elegance (notably Natchez and New Orleans) and indirectly fuelled the textile dominance of Lancashire. However, slavery spread everywhere across the 'Black Belt', which stretched from Georgia across Alabama and Mississippi (Map 71).

The net result of the cotton revolution was the transfer of slavery across huge tracts of North America. Whereas in the mid-eighteenth century slavery was rooted in concentrated areas in eastern colonies, with a toehold on the Gulf coast and Florida, a century later slavery had seeped westwards, through West Virginia and into Missouri, and it stretched as far west as the Texas border with New Mexico. Slavery may not have been the cause of the Civil War (and four slave states did not secede from the Union), but the battle lines unfolded along the slave/freedom axis (Maps 72 and 73).

At the outbreak of the Civil War, the USA was home to four million slaves, which represented a massive increase on the half a million or so who had become American citizens, of a sort, at independence in 1776. Their numbers had not grown from a transatlantic importation of Africans (the engine behind the increase of the populations of the Caribbean and Brazil – and the Old South); they had grown *naturally*. States from the older settled Atlantic seaboard, with expanding black populations, were able to supply the demands of planters and slave traders in the new states and settlements on the cotton frontier (Maps 74 and 75).

The USA no longer needed Africa. But it *did* need a slave trade. Those coffles of slaves moving by foot and boat across the face of settled North America form some of the most disturbing of American images. This was the period of heightened slave distress, when the agonies of slavery were often compounded by family separations, with families split by slave traders trawling for suitable

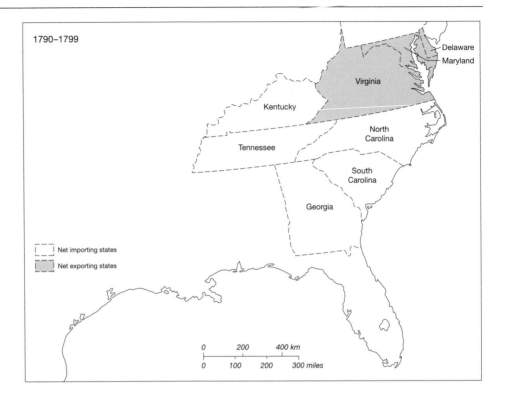

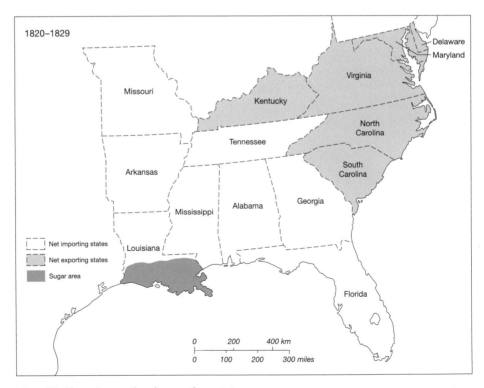

Map 71 Slave-importing/exporting states

Source: After Tadman, Michael. *Speculators and Slaves*, p. 6. © 1989. Reprinted by permission of The University of Wisconsin Press.

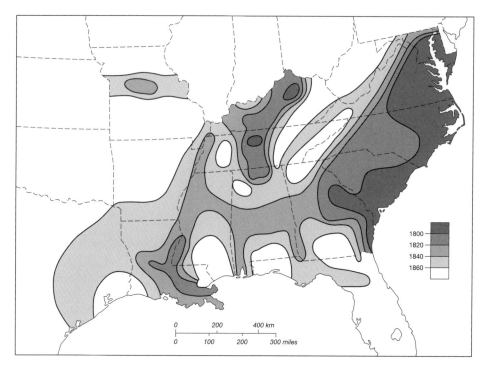

Map 72 The frontier areas with significant slave numbers, 1800–1860

Source: After *Dictionary of Afro-American Slavery* edited by R. M. Miller and J. D. Smith. Copyright © 1988 by Randall M. Miller and John David Smith. Reproduced with permission of Greenwood Publishing Group, Inc., Westport, CT.

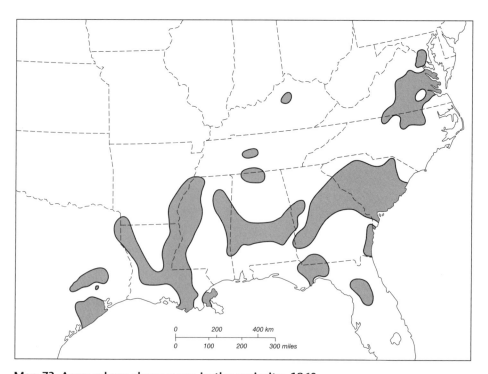

Map 73 Areas where slaves were in the majority, 1860

Source: After *Dictionary of Afro-American Slavery* edited by R. M. Miller and J. D. Smith. Copyright © 1988 by Randall M. Miller and John David Smith. Reproduced with permission of Greenwood Publishing Group, Inc., Westport, CT.

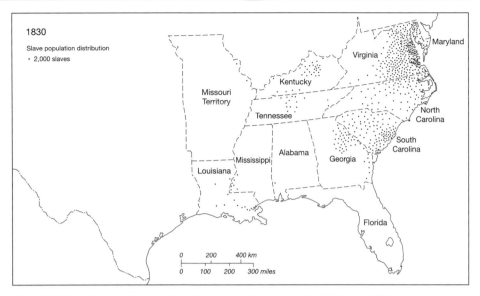

Map 74 The distribution of the slave population in the USA, c. 1830
Source: Copyright © 1999. From *The Routledge Historical Atlas of the American South* by A. K. Frank. Reproduced by permission of Routledge/Taylor & Francis Books, Inc.

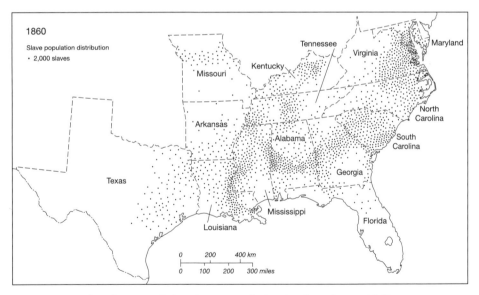

Map 75 The distribution of the slave population in the USA, c. 1860
Source: Copyright © 1999. From *The Routledge Historical Atlas of the American South* by A. K. Frank. Reproduced by permission of Routledge/Taylor & Francis Books, Inc.

labour to buy and move to the cotton states. The agonies wrought by this internal American slave trade were there for all to see.

At independence in 1776, North America had inherited slavery from the British, but by the outbreak of the Civil War, slavery had become a distinctive North American institution, and problem. It crumbled in the violence of the Civil War: emancipation came via the Thirteenth Amendment of 1865 (Map 76).

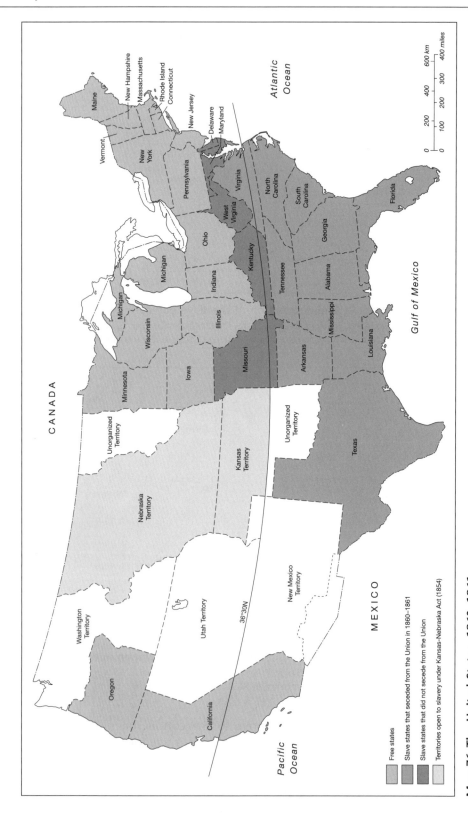

Map 76 The United States, 1860–1861

Source: After Rodriguez, J. P. (1999) *Chronology of World Slavery*, ABC-CLIO, p. xxxi.

CHAPTER 17

Slave resistance

The history of slavery is the history of slave resistance. Indeed, we know a great deal about slavery from the attempts by slave holders to keep slaves in their place: laws to regulate slaves, to punish the recalcitrant and innumerable examples of punishments meted out to resistant slaves. In recent years, however, historians have begun to discuss slave resistance more subtly and to argue that resistance involved much more than revolt or rebellion. It has also become clear that a great deal of slave resistance derived directly from the slaves' African past.

Slaves resisted their bondage in many different ways – most spectacularly, and best remembered, by open revolt. The great Roman slave revolt led by Spartacus in 73–71 BC remains perhaps the best-remembered slave revolt (if only because of the epic savagery subsequently meted out to the defeated slaves, crucified in their thousands by the Romans). More common was everyday resistance: truculence, incomprehension and foot dragging – anything short of open defiance. Slaves always trod a delicate line between having to obey and to do what was expected of them (or risk punishment) and not doing it too eagerly or thoroughly. It was a fundamental lesson passed on by slave parents to their offspring: to learn how to tread that delicate line between essential obedience and minimal cooperation. For their part, slave owners everywhere complained about their slaves: about their indolence, their stupidity, and their failure to grasp essential points and to do their work promptly and efficiently. Such failings (in slave owners' eyes) were part of the slavish condition. For the slaves, it was a social and labouring culture of resistance that made their lives a little more tolerable.

More obvious – and a major refrain in the literature of Atlantic slave societies – was the runaway slave. Slave runaways were to be found in all slave societies. In many they formed distinct (maroon) communities of runaways that, in time, developed their own identity and power. In remote frontier or inaccessible areas, they held out for long periods against hostile planters and European military. Such communities were generally African-dominated, sometimes guerilla-like and always separate from local mainstream slave life. The British fought a protracted war against maroons in Jamaica, but the most successful were the 'Bush Negro' communities in the tropical forests of Suriname. Similarly in Brazil, the maroon community of Palmares in Alagoas survived throughout most of the seventeenth century. When it finally surrendered in 1697, its leader Zumbi and his followers committed mass suicide. But it was only the most spectacular of a large number of such communities, many to be found in the sugar region of Bahia.

More persistent and widespread were the simple acts of escape. Individual slaves ran away from brutality, from a hated master/mistress, sometimes for a few days away from life's troubles (though they generally faced more trouble on return). More likely, however, slave fugitives were running away *to* someone: to a partner or lover, to parents or children, to relatives or friends. Sometimes they covered great distances (and were clearly sustained by other slaves on their risky and arduous journeys) and sometimes for long periods.

Slave holders feared their slaves. They worried what the slaves might do to them. And this had begun on the African coast and on the slave ships (Map 77). We know for example of at least 493 slave revolts on board Atlantic slave ships, to say nothing of smaller incidents and acts of violence against white slave traders. The shipboard Africans were heavily manacled and carefully guarded by armed men for very good reasons. The same fears continued to haunt slave owners throughout the Americas: they could never guarantee their slaves' obedience or passivity. Slaves might – and did – strike back without hint or warning. They could harm (or kill) their owners and children in their homes, hurt their animals, damage their properties. Slave owners were quick to suspect plots and dangers: when they fell sick they often assumed it was the work of a mischievous or plotting slave. Sometimes they were right; more often, however, their suspicions were a reflection of their innate fears of the sullen black community that surrounded them and about which they knew so little (even when they shared daily living space).

Most spectacular of all forms of slave resistance were slave revolts and rebellions. Only one fully succeeded in overthrowing slave society: the Haitian revolt of 1791. Most failed and were crushed, normally with a savage brutality designed to overawe other slaves. Yet a great variety of revolts, some with minimal aims, others with vaunting ambitions, flared across the enslaved Americas. Though revolts in North America rarely approached the size or threat of those to be found in the heavily African slave societies of the Caribbean islands or Brazil, North American slave owners found them no less terrifying and threatening. Depending on definitions, there is information on sixty-five North American revolts, but there were many other plots and alarms (for the whites). Bacon's rebellion in Virginia in 1676 saw rebellious slaves unite with disaffected indentured whites. In South Carolina in 1739, Stono's rebellion was grouped around twenty rebellious Angolan slaves keen to escape to Spanish Florida. After the Pointe Coupee slave rebellion in Louisiana in 1795, twenty-six slaves were hanged. The upheavals continued to pockmark the story of North American slavery, notably Gabriel Prosser's in Virginia (1800), Denmark Vesey, South Carolina (1822) and Nat Turner, also Virginia in 1831 (Map 78). The victims of these revolts, and the defeated slaves, suffered ugly fates, but the numbers involved, and the levels of violence, paled when compared with the endemic violence of slave revolts in the West Indies. Among the most memorable were Tackey's revolt in Antigua (1735–1736), another Tackey's revolt in Jamaica in 1760, Fedon's rebellion in Grenada (1795–1797), which were all crushed in the field or via the courts with a bloody retribution designed both to crush the insurgents and to horrify survivors. The blood letting between black and white reached a crescendo in the British islands between 1816 and freedom in 1834: Bussa's

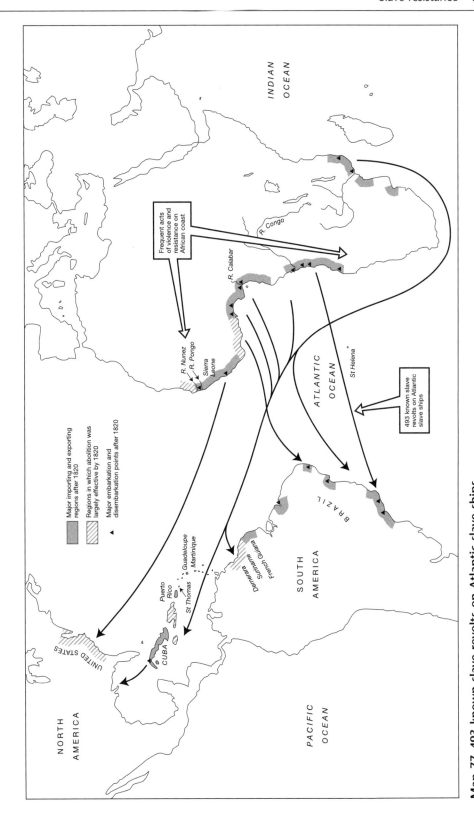

Map 77 493 known slave revolts on Atlantic slave ships

Source: Adapted from Eltis, D. and Walvin, J. (eds) (1981) *The Abolition of the Atlantic Slave Trade*, University of Wisconsin Press.

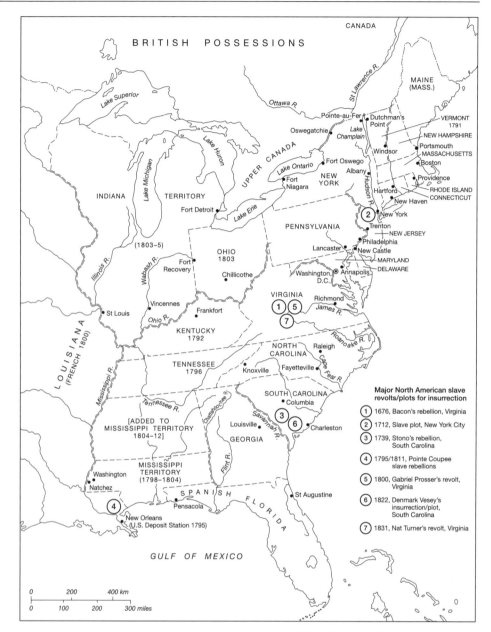

Map 78 Major North American slave revolts and plotted insurrections
Source: Adapted from *The American Heritage Pictorial Atlas of US History* (1966), American Heritage
Publishing Company.

rebellion in Barbados (1816), the slave revolt in Demerara (Guyana) in 1823,
and finally the 'Baptist War' in Jamaica 1831–32. All were brought to a climax of
such excessive blood letting that British public opinion swung decisively against
slavery itself (Map 79).

But all this was as nothing when set against the seismic upheaval that destroyed
slavery in St Domingue and ushered in the black republic of Haiti between 1791

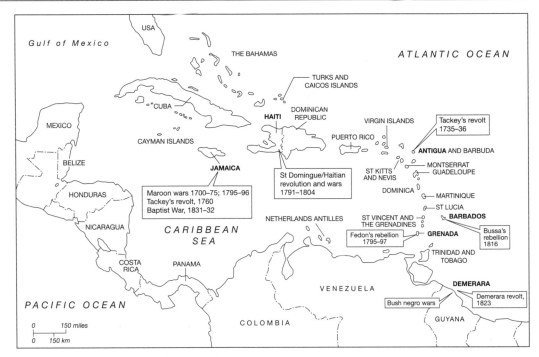

Map 79 Major Caribbean slave revolts
Source: Adapted from Rogozinski, J. (1994) *A Brief History of the Caribbean: From the Arawak and the Carib to the Present*, Meridian Books, p. 294. © 1994 by Jan Rogozinski.

and 1804. The Haitian revolt destroyed the local slave system, devoured the invading armies of France, Spain and Britain and sent terrified refugees scattering in panic throughout the Caribbean and to North America. The Haitian revolt sent a tremor of fear throughout slave society across the Americas.

Yet slavery lived on in the nineteenth century, especially in Spanish America and Brazil, where slaves persisted in their acts of resistance and rebellion. In Brazil, where slavery was much harsher and more violent and where slaves were more resistant than earlier historians had imagined, resistance was again a feature of slave life. From maroon communities to rebellions (especially in the last phase of Brazilian slavery in the 1880s), Brazilian slaves did what they could to confront slavery and to make it less oppressive. And this was true in all kinds of slave work, from the mines of Minas Gerais to the new coffee plantations of southern Brazil (Map 80).

Brazil was by far the largest slave society in the Americas: it received more Africans, over a longer period, than any other. Its remarkable size and geographical diversity ensured that some features of local slavery (and of slave resistance) would be peculiar to Brazil, but the similarities with the slave experience elsewhere are even more striking. Brazilian slaves ran away in large numbers, and there were more maroon communities in Brazil than anywhere else in the Americas. Bahia – centre of the sugar industry and closest in sailing time to the slave markets of Africa – was the location of the largest concentration/number of Brazilian slave revolts in the years between 1807 and 1835 (the years when

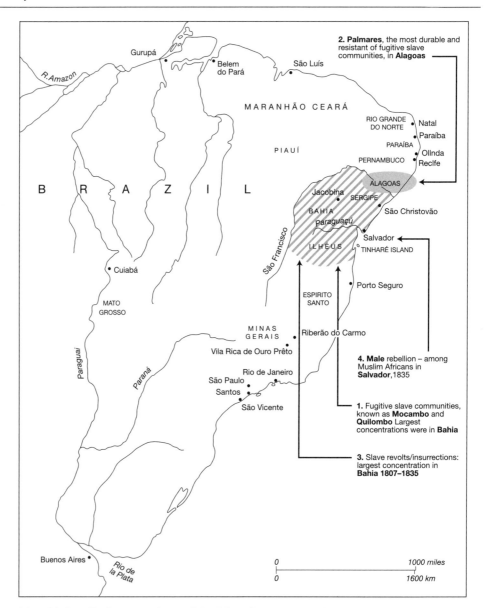

Map 80 Brazil: slave revolts and fugitive slave communities
Source: Adapted from Schwartz, S. B. (1985) *Sugar Plantations in the Formation of Brazilian Society: Bahia, 1550–1835*, Cambridge University Press, p. 21.

huge numbers of Africans were imported into Brazil). And it was there that the remarkable revolt, the Male, erupted among Islamic Africans in 1835. There, as in other parts of the Americas, revolt was grounded in African cultures and an African past. In maroon societies, in revolt, as in myriad cultural forms of slave life, Africa remained the defining element. The story of slave resistance is a reminder that the cultures of the enslaved Americas lead us back, time and again, to the source of that enslaved humanity – to Africa.

CHAPTER 18

Abolition and emancipation

The campaign to end the slave trade and slavery has puzzled historians perhaps more than any other aspect of the history of slavery. For centuries, the Atlantic slave trade had grown and thrived with very little intellectual or economic opposition, yet by the end of the eighteenth century, powerful abolitionist groups and movements had taken root on both sides of the English-speaking Atlantic. The origins of anti-slavery were complex and international, drawing upon ideas from the Enlightenment and the Age of Revolutions and finding sustenance in the transformation of the world of dissent in the eighteenth century. Despite the pioneering efforts of American abolitionists, the centre of abolitionist sentiment and organization was Britain. In the early nineteenth century, British abolitionism became the engine behind the drive to abolish slavery worldwide. Indeed, global abolition became a distinctively British passion throughout the nineteenth century, yet this in itself is a historical curiosity, because in the course of the eighteenth century the British had become the *greatest* slave traders in the Atlantic: a century later, they prided themselves on their abolitionist credentials.

Throughout much of its history, few people had questioned Atlantic slavery. From roughly 1776, however, it attracted a growing chorus of criticism. One critical strand emerged from the doubts about human bondage sown by Enlightenment writing. Equally, the 'Age of Revolutions' (with its emphasis on rights and equality), beginning with American independence in 1776 and culminating in the French Revolution of 1789, proved corrosive to slavery. It was a process that gathered pace after the Haitian slave revolt of 1791.

In Britain and North America, the critical initial role was played by Quakers, who had opposed slavery from the late seventeenth century and had been among the first to do so. Though relatively few in numbers, Quakers were hugely influential. Articulate, literate and prosperous, with a thriving print culture and well-primed national organizations, Quakers in Philadelphia and London were the key force behind the creation of abolitionist organizations in the 1780s.

In Britain, abolition blossomed after 1787, quickly developing a national and widely popular base. It also secured an important position in the House of Commons. The initial abolitionist goal was to end the Atlantic slave trade, and although the circumstances of revolution and war (after 1793) delayed the campaign, abolition of the slave trade was achieved in 1807. At a stroke, the major Atlantic slave traders – the British – ended their oceanic trade in Africans. So too did the Americans. However, slavery itself continued, both in the British West Indies and in the USA, though now detached from the old supply lines to African humanity.

British abolitionists hoped that by cutting off the supplies of Africans, planters would be forced to improve their treatment of slaves and that, in some indefinable way, they would come to recognize the greater efficiencies of free labour and would move away from slavery. That did not happen, however. To discover exactly what was happening to the slave populations after abolition, British abolitionists instituted slave 'Registration' (1813), a census of slaves in the Caribbean islands that would reveal important demographic data. Counting heads was the surest way of assessing the impact of abolition (and also of checking if planters were importing Africans illegally). For their part, planters clung to slavery with even greater resolve and showed no sign of giving it up. Thus, from 1823 onwards, a new abolitionist campaign was launched to end slavery itself. As before, it was a campaign that rallied massive popular support and pressured Parliament from both within and without. This time it sought an end to slavery itself. Anti-slavery was greatly helped by what was happening in the slave islands. A number of slave revolts (Barbados 1816, Demerara 1823 and Jamaica 1831–32), with their savage, bloody repression, provided regular reminders (if any were needed) of the savagery that lay at the heart of colonial slavery. Moreover, the rapid dissemination of Christianity among the slaves (and missionaries' reports of Christian slaves being persecuted) fuelled widespread British outrage against Caribbean slavery.

The final push for black freedom was greatly helped by the Reform Act of 1832 and by the consequent change in the composition of the House of Commons (though the Lords remained stubbornly pro-slavery). The reformed Parliament was now sympathetic towards abolition. Freedom was granted to 750,000 slaves in the British West Indies, partly in 1833, fully in 1838, but it was granted only by paying slave owners a staggering £20 million in compensation. In effect, Parliament had bought the slaves' freedom.

The ex-slaves and their former owners celebrated black freedom on both sides of the Atlantic. For their part, the British and the spokesmen for the old planter interests soon came to realize that in some former slave colonies, black freedom had created a labour shortage. To fill the gaps created by those former slaves who, when possible, quit the plantations for freedom on their own lands, the British devised a new form of bondage. Indentured labour had been widely used in the early colonial settlements but was now tried again, using Indian labour, throughout the Caribbean and in other colonial settlements in the Indian Ocean, Africa and later in the Pacific. The result was an extraordinary migration of labouring people from their Indian homelands. By the time indentured labour was ended after the First World War, almost 1.5 million Indians had been shipped from India by the colonial power that trumpeted its virtue in abolishing slavery.

Stiffened by their victory in 1833, British abolitionists henceforth embarked on a global abolition campaign using the unchallenged power of the Royal Navy in the Atlantic and Indian Oceans and harnessing the influence of the Foreign Office and diplomacy to persuade the rest of the world to follow Britain's recent example. Not everyone was happy or willing to comply with Britain's moral threats, not least because, in places, there was still profit to be made from both slavery and slave trading (notably, for example, in supplying Brazil and Cuba).

Indian overseas labour emigration, 1834–1924

Principal destinations	Indentured	Free of indenture
Mauritius, 1834–1910	455,187	
Réunion, 1841–82	74,854	
British Guiana, 1838–1918	238,861	
Trinidad, 1845–1917	149,623	
Jamaica, 1845–1915	38,595	
Other British West Indies, 1838–1915	11,152	
French Caribbean, 1853–85	79,089	
Dutch Guiana, 1873–1916	34,503	
East Africa, 1895–1922	39,437	
Natal, 1860–1911	152,932	
Fiji, 1879–1916	61,015	
Burma, 1852–1924		1,164,000
Ceylon, 1843–1924		2,321,000
British Malaya, 1844–1910	13,000	1,624,000
Total	1,465,248	5,109,000

Europeans were understandably suspicious of British intentions. The British had recently thrived on slavery but now, when they were industrializing rapidly and were apparently able to prosper by a different economic route, they demanded that all other nations should follow their abolitionist example, ideally by diplomatic persuasion, otherwise by naval enforcement. Whatever the cause, abolition quickly spread among Europe's slave-owning and slave-trading nations. As with the British, the maritime slave trade succumbed before slavery itself. Throughout continental Europe, there was no political movement to compare with the broadly based popular abolitionist campaigns in Britain. European politics, especially popular urban politics, were different. Consequently, European abolition tended to be played out not as a theme in popular politics but as a debate within governing circles. No local popular process was brought to bear to force governments to end their colonial slave systems. Instead, European governments faced regular and mounting pressure from the British. Much as it was generally resented (as a form of British interference), British abolitionist pressure in Europe proved successful. Eventually, European powers succumbed, one by one, and brought their slave systems to an end.

As with Britain, the slave trade ended before colonial slavery itself. By 1815, Sweden, Denmark and the Netherlands had already ended their trade in African slaves. However, France persisted with its own trade until 1830. Brazil's thriving slave system continued to attract Portuguese slave traders until abolition was imposed in 1850. Spain finally complied in 1867. However, slavery itself lingered on in European colonial possessions. Sweden emancipated its slaves in 1847, Denmark the year after and the Netherlands in 1863. However, Spain clung on to slavery until 1870–1873 in Puerto Rico and, finally, in Cuba until 1886. Revolutionary France had abolished slavery in 1794 but had reintroduced it in 1802, finally emancipating its slaves in 1848 (Map 81).

The story of the ending of US slavery is well known. American slavery thrived on cotton until the outbreak of the Civil War. Despite an extraordinary

Map 81 Major slave emancipations

Source: Adapted from Rogozinski, J. (1994) *A Brief History of the Caribbean: From the Arawak and the Carib to the Present*, Meridian Books, p. 294. © 1994 by Jan Rogozinski.

'underground railroad' that moved slaves northwards to freedom, the rising influence of northern abolition sentiment and organization (much influenced again by the British) was thwarted by the economic vitality of slave-grown cotton (Map 82). Many had come to feel that slavery was a necessary evil. Without the Civil War, there seems little reason to doubt that slavery would have continued. American abolitionists also faced violent opposition to their activities, especially in the slave-owning South, but all this came to a dramatic end with the Civil War. Though the war was not *caused* by slavery, the war spelled the end of slavery in the USA – eventually. Lincoln issued the Emancipation Proclamation in 1863, and in 1865 the Thirteenth Amendment to the Constitution finally outlawed slavery in the USA.

Slavery in other parts of the Americas was eroded by many of the abolitionist forces we have seen at work elsewhere: changes in cultural values unleashed by the Enlightenment; the upheavals set in train by the French Revolution; and especially by the Haitian slave revolt and the political pressure exerted by the British. Equally, and again as in Britain, the influence of modernization, especially industrial change, served to diminish the economic effectiveness of slavery (and its rationale). Wage labour had established itself as a better (more viable, more profitable and more easily justified) system than slavery. In Latin America, anti-slavery was also entangled in the local struggle for independence from Spain.

Throughout South America (excepting Brazil and Cuba), the end of the Atlantic slave trade cut off local slave populations from old African supply routes.

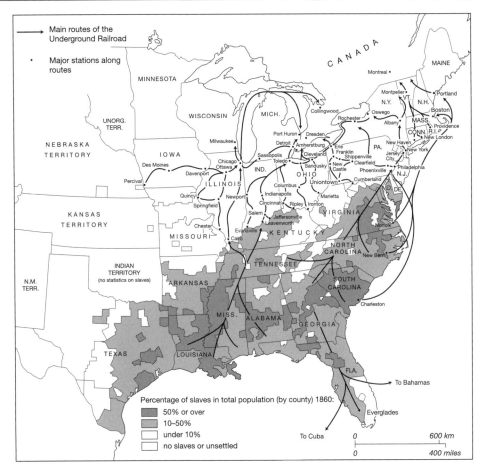

Map 82 Slaves and the 'underground railroad', 1840–1860
Source: After *The American Heritage Pictorial Atlas of US History* (1966), American Heritage Publishing Company.

It also served to diminish the local slave populations and thereby minimize their economic importance. And everywhere, slaves themselves struck out against slavery, notably through acts of resistance and rebellion. Moreover, all this took place in a political climate that was increasingly influenced by strident abolitionism, often orchestrated by the British. The cumulative effect was the gradual erosion of will among slave owners and the parallel strengthened determination among abolitionists that slavery was doomed – and must be ended. Still, it was a protracted affair which lasted until the ending of Brazilian slavery in 1888.

Of course, slavery was not equally important throughout the Americas. Where slavery was marginal, it was quickly eliminated. This was the case in Chile in 1823 and Mexico in 1829. Between 1842–1855 there followed a plethora of emancipations (Uruguay, Bolivia, Colombia, Ecuador, Argentina, Venezuela and Peru). Brazil, as we have seen elsewhere, struggled on until 1888. In the Spanish Caribbean Puerto Rico's slavery was ended between 1870–1873, but Cuba held out until 1886. In both cases, the issue was complicated by the resistance of

Madrid and by the Spanish attachment, in the teeth of British-American opposition, to the slave trade until the 1860s.

In the fifty-plus years which separated British from Brazilian emancipation (1833–1888) the Americas were cleansed of their slave systems. They had, however, proved remarkably durable, mainly because they had yielded such material benefits. Once slavery had taken root, it could not easily be uprooted, even under changing economic circumstance. Slavery took on a life of its own. Slave owners became attached to the broader slave-owning culture, and could rarely envisage a future without slaves. Slaves on the other hand had persistently sought, despite their persecution, to resist bondage as best they could. Throughout, there was the increasingly strident voice of abolitionists, often inspired or manipulated by the British, nagging away in the cause of black freedom worldwide and serving, ultimately, to erode both the confidence in, and the justifications for, slavery. Slavery in the Americas started slowly and unpredictably, and was brought to an end in an equally piecemeal fashion.

CHAPTER 19

East Africa and the Indian Ocean

There had been ancient slave routes within and from East Africa, and a slave trade in that vast region continued down to the modern era. A trade in slaves had thrived between ancient Egypt and African societies to the south: we know for example of African slaves in Alexandria in the second century AD. Slaves were shipped between Somalia and Egypt. Others were transported eastwards from Africa to Arabia and even on to India. This slave trade from East Africa had accelerated with the spread of Islam and with the consequent establishment of Arab slave posts along the East African coast. Thus, when Europeans first sailed into the region in the late fifteenth century, they encountered existing slaving systems and slave communities much as they had in West Africa. They also found slavery much further afield (Map 83).

Long before the Portuguese arrived, there were African slaves and communities descended from slaves (most likely of Abyssinian descent) scattered across India, from the north to Ceylon. We know for example of fifteenth-century Indian rulers who made widespread use of Africans as soldiers in their armies: Africans were also noticeable in a number of Indian navies. From the fifteenth century onwards, however, both Islamic and Portuguese traders carried Africans to India. Most of the slaves in the new African-based communities along the west coast of India were engaged in domestic work, though some individuals rose to prominence as traders. However, these slaves did not have the same chattel status as African slaves in the Americas. As a major Portuguese trading empire developed in India, with important Portuguese slave-trading links to West Africa and on to Brazil, it was inevitable that Africans would pass along Portugal's trading routes and become more noticeable in the Portuguese posts in India. Again, the Africans tended to occupy servile roles, understandably perhaps given the role of Africans as slaves in the broader Portuguese empire. However, it is perhaps more surprising to learn that the transportation of slaves out of East Africa continued into the nineteenth century.[1]

The nineteenth-century boom in East African slaves was inspired mainly by the domestic slave markets of Arabia: Mecca and Medina, for example, absorbed between 15,000 and 20,000 slaves each year. Furthermore, the movement of slaves *into* East Africa from the African interior was also encouraged by the development of slave-based plantations (producing cloves, coconuts and grain) along the East African coast. In fact, a majority of all these East African captives remained enslaved *within* Africa. It has been calculated that in the nineteenth century

[1] Ann M. Pescatello, 'The African presence in Portuguese India', in Patrick Manning (ed.), *Slave Trade 1500–1800*, Aldershot, 1996, Ch.7.

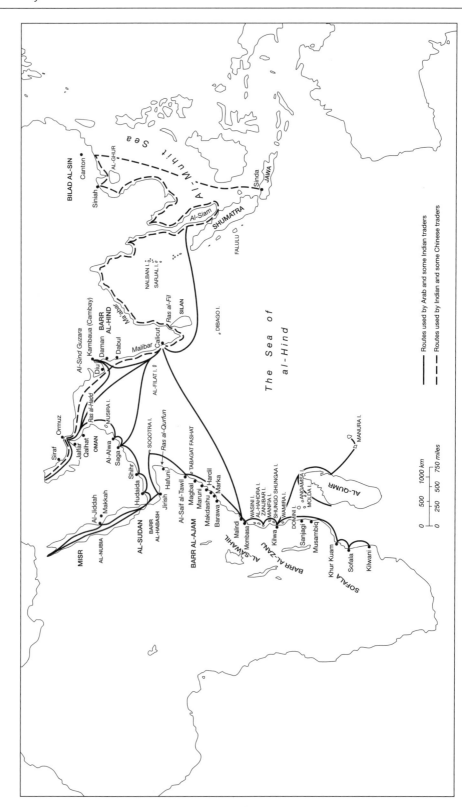

Map 83 East African trade in the Indian Ocean, c. 1500
Source: After Freeman-Grenville, G. S. P. *The New Atlas of African History*, R. G. Collings, p. 75.

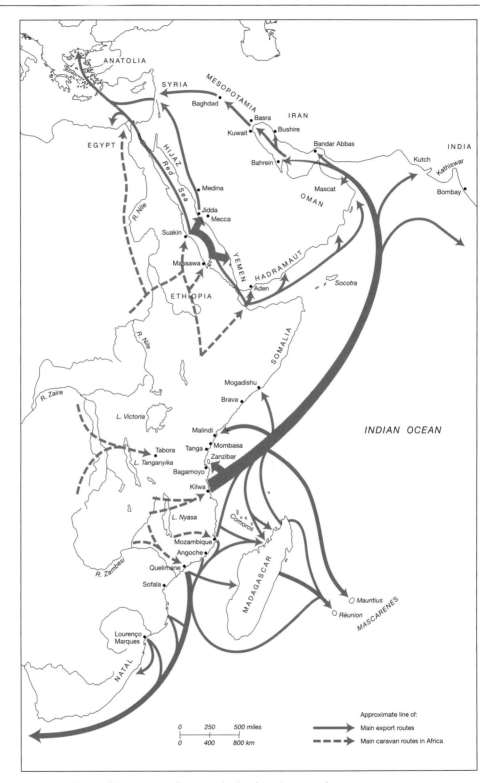

Map 84 The Indian Ocean slave trade in the nineteenth century

Source: After Clarence-Smith, W. G. (ed.) (1989) *The Economy of the Indian Ocean Slave Trade*, Frank Cass, p. 2.

alone, perhaps 1.5 million slaves were moved along these East African slave routes.[2] It is difficult to be precise about the overall numbers involved, but the total number of slaves caught up in the East African slave trade has been calculated at upwards of five million people (Map 84).

This massive movement of Africans into slavery has often been overlooked because of the scholarly and popular concentration on the Atlantic slave trade. Moreover, like the slave trade on the West African coast, the East African trade had major repercussions in the African interior. Over the course of the nineteenth century, armies of Africans were forcibly removed from their homelands in the interior towards the East African coast – and far beyond, though the numbers began to decline late in the century under the pressure of British diplomacy and military might. However, it forms an important reminder that slavery continued long after abolition.

[2] Paul Lovejoy, *Transformations in Slavery*, Cambridge, 1983, p.151.

CHAPTER 20

Slavery after abolition

Over the course of the nineteenth century, anti-slavery (abolition) seemed to be universally triumphant. Slavery was brought to an end across the Americas and was challenged around the world by zealous British abolitionists. The most important anti-slavery organization was British, founded initially in 1787 and given new form in 1839 when it took the name the British and Foreign Anti-Slavery Society. The British anti-slavery campaigns were critical not merely within the British Empire but globally, by pressing the anti-slavery cause on all and sundry – whether they liked it or not. In fact, anti-slavery became a key element in a cultural imperialism that characterized British foreign (and military) policy for large stretches of the nineteenth century. The British took great pride in their anti-slavery credentials and achievements and felt confident enough to lecture all other nations and peoples on the need to accord to the high abolitionist standards set by the British themselves. In the same period, however, the British were much less forthcoming about their own slaving past.

They were especially reluctant to address the influential role that the British had played between roughly 1660 and 1800 in ferrying unprecedented numbers of Africans across the Atlantic and in grounding their Caribbean empire and prosperity in the labour of African slaves. After a fashion, the triumph and power of British anti-slavery in the nineteenth century served as a smokescreen to mask the earlier episode of British slavery. It was as if abolition had wiped the historical slate clean, but of course it had not. Nor had it triumphed as completely and universally as it imagined. This is confirmed by one simple fact: the British and Foreign Anti-Slavery Society of 1839 survives to this day, albeit under a different, more appropriately modern name, Anti-Slavery International. The society's aims are the same, of confronting and undermining slavery in all corners of the globe. Despite the great anti-slavery triumphs of the nineteenth century – the purging of the Americas of those slave systems introduced and perfected by Europeans and settlers, and the continuing attacks on slavery in Africa and India – slavery survived, thrived even.

To a marked degree, modern-day campaigns against slavery have sustained themselves, and generated public support, by their insistence on redefining slavery itself. Historians have long wrestled with the definition of slavery: what exactly *is* it, and how has it differed from place to place and across time? Simply to concentrate on chattel slavery – the fundamental type of slavery that emerged in the Americas – would be to overlook a host of gross human violations and denials of freedom that blight the lives of millions of people the world over, right down to the present day. Modern research into the extent and ubiquity of child labour, sex slavery and human trafficking, in addition to chattel slavery, has revealed astonishing evidence. Anti-Slavery International has shown that, today, there are twenty million bonded labourers around the world and 246 million child labourers, while something like 800,000 people are trafficked internationally against their will *each year*. No country on Earth admits to the legality of slavery today – but large numbers tolerate it. Perhaps this is not surprising in the light of the extent of world poverty (an estimated two billion people living on less than two dollars a day).[1] Such data have understandably aroused public and political concern, but they also serve to remind us that contemporary anti-slavery campaigns, whatever their past achievements, continue to face a daunting task.

If the nineteenth century seemed to present a series of anti-slavery triumphs, the twentieth century offers a contrasting, dismal story. Although it was a century that saw, from the halfway mark, the rapid collapse of most of the old empires that had sustained a number of major human injustices, the century was also characterized by inhumanities on a staggering and unprecedented scale. Indeed, the major human catastrophes of the 1930s and 1940s involved the reintroduction of slavery and the destruction of humanity on a scale that dwarfed most earlier epochs – and all in a very short space of time. Two regimes stand out: Stalinist Russia and Nazi Germany. Though not the only offenders, those regimes, in different ways and under different guises, resorted to slavery. Both dragooned millions of peoples (their own citizens and outsiders) for the physical advancement of the regime, for territorial and economic expansion – and to wage war. Slave labour became a dominant characteristic of both Nazi and Stalinist regimes – and this was in addition to the industrialized slaughter perfected by the Nazis. Slave labour camps were dotted across Nazi Europe, and the Gulag of the massive Russian empire devoured untold millions of people. Even after years of careful research, the statistics remain uncertain, but the broad impression is undisputed. Millions of Russian citizens simply vanished into Stalin's vast slave labour camps of the Gulag empire (along with others in satellite communist states in Eastern and Central Europe). Wholesale removal of populations accounted for millions more: some 1.5 million Muslims, and perhaps five million peasants for example (Maps 85 and 86). The millions of European Jews uprooted from their various homelands by the Nazis and transported to camps where they were subsequently slaughtered (Map 87), remain the most infamous of many groups similarly uprooted, transported and destroyed. Nazi Germany fought the Second World War on the backs of millions of slave labourers (most imported), upwards perhaps of twelve million, at least 2.5 million of whom survive to this day to the accompaniment of massive legal cases against the German state and German industries. Such staggering figures, even allowing for statistical uncertainties, and the endemic problem (in discussing slavery) of definition tend to blunt the senses. It also seems bizarre that the war between those two nations was made possible to a marked degree by their respective use of slave labour.

[1] See Anti-Slavery International website: www.antislavery.org. Also *National Geographic*, September 2003, '21st Century Slaves'.

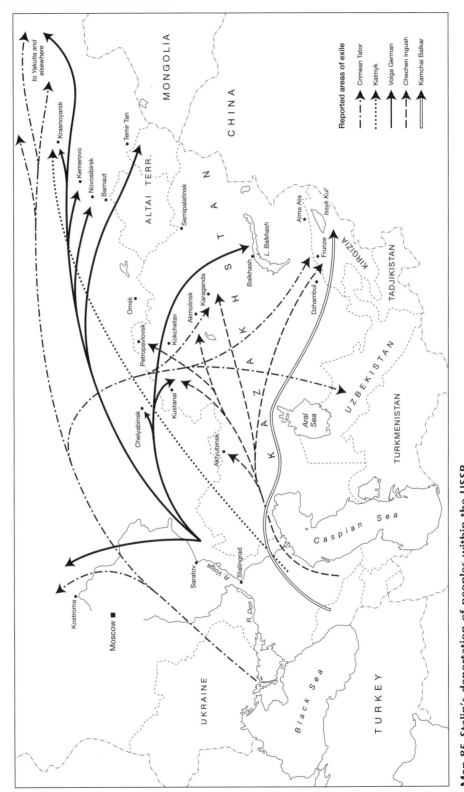

Map 85 Stalin's deportation of peoples within the USSR

Source: After Conquest, R. (1966) *The Nation Killers: The Soviet Deportation of Nationalities*, Macmillan, p. 96.

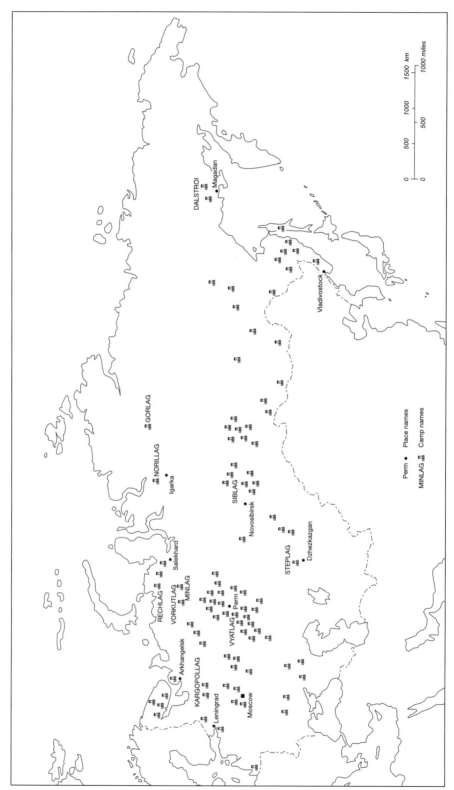

Map 86 The Russian Gulag

Source: Adapted from *Gulag: A History of the Soviet Camps* by Anne Applebaum, copyright © 2003 by Anne Applebaum. Used by permission of Doubleday, a division of Random House, Inc. Reproduced by permission of Penguin Books Ltd., pp. 120–21.

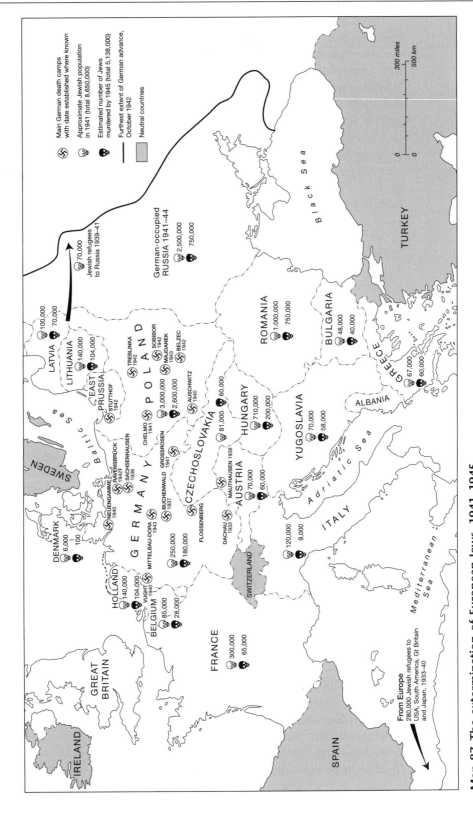

Map 87 The extermination of European Jews, 1941–1945

Source: © Martin Gilbert. After *Recent History Atlas: 1870 to the Present Day* by Martin Gilbert, published in the UK by Weidenfeld 1966, p. 86. Reprinted by permission of Routledge and Sir Martin Gilbert.

The examples of Stalinist Russia and Nazi Germany present a hugely puzzling problem: why did sophisticated, modern societies revert to slavery, to labour systems that the Western world had long ago denounced and rejected? By the mid-nineteenth century, proponents of slavery were in retreat throughout the Western world, though US slavery survived until given the *coup de grâce* by the Civil War. Yet a century later, slavery had re-emerged, *and* on an even greater scale: the slave systems of the twentieth century involved even *more* people than had been ensnared in the Americas. Moreover, all was accompanied by a mechanized savagery that overshadowed even the worst excesses of Atlantic slavery. Furthermore, in the twentieth century slavery was to be found not in distant settlements, or in the far-flung corners of European empires, but in Europe itself: throughout the expanse of Nazi-occupied Europe and across the vast tracts of Stalin's empire. Anti-slavery may have felt successfully triumphant in, say, 1865, but who, a century on, could feel so sanguine when looking back at the massive human suffering of the twentieth century?

The example of twentieth-century slavery and human destruction has cast a recent shadow over the study of slavery. First, it has forced historians to rethink earlier episodes of human bondage. More influentially, perhaps, as the full horrors of totalitarian regimes have unfolded, the evidence has provided political critics of slavery with a ready-made set of examples and comparisons, and even a new vocabulary, to apply to earlier slave systems. This has been most striking in the use of the term 'Holocaust'. Atlantic slavery, but especially the Middle Passage, is now regularly described as 'the African Holocaust'. It is an eye-catching and memorable phrase (which may explain why it has been adopted and accepted so quickly and so widely), yet in many critical respects it is also misleading and inappropriate. Unlike the Holocaust, which consumed European Jewry, Atlantic slavery was not genocidal in intent or outcome. For all its brutality, the aim of Atlantic slavery was to get as many Africans into the Americas as swiftly and as cheaply as possible. In the process, there was suffering on an epic scale, but as Herbert Klein reminds us, the majority of Africans loaded on to the slave ships survived and landed in the Americas – however wretched their condition, and however bleak their immediate prospects. Europe's Jews did not survive.

The linking of the Jewish Holocaust to the experience of African slaves has opened another more overtly political issue. The state of Israel and Nazi survivors have been able to force the German state to pay massive reparations for the damage and destruction wrought on Jewry. More recently, even the Russian Duma has compensated Russian victims of the Gulag. If reparations should be paid for the European (Jewish) Holocaust, why not for another (the African)? Thus the comparative vocabulary – the use of the term 'Holocaust' in these two very different cases – has provided strength to the demand for reparations for slavery. Those who put forward demands for slave reparations (especially in the USA) have developed complex and persuasive arguments. But the case was initially inspired and sustained by the model of the Jewish Holocaust and Israel.

Whatever the pros and cons of the reparations argument, the debate has helped to bring slavery centre stage. Unlike most other historical topics, slavery finds itself at the centre of a broadly based contemporary social and political debate – and not simply in academic circles. Even among academics, the study of slavery has been transformed. A mere generation ago, slavery was a marginal subject among Western historians. Since the mid-1960s, however, there has been a massive expansion in slave studies. Today, it is widely accepted that slavery was a critical element in the shaping of the modern Western world. Atlantic slavery attracts the attention of huge numbers of historians, and publications about each and every feature of slavery spill off the presses. The teaching of slavery reflects this shift and now forms an important component in most colleges and universities on both sides of the Atlantic. All this is in addition to a massive growth in *public* awareness about slavery. In large part, this popular memory has been cultivated by public history: by museums, galleries, exhibitions, plantation tours (each year millions of people visit slave sites on US plantations, for example) not to mention popular novels, films, TV and radio. There is no clear dividing line between academic history and public history, for the popular media draws heavily on academic work, but this expansion of knowledge about slavery, in academic and popular cultural forms, has edged slavery to the centre of popular awareness.

There has never been any need to remind people descended from slaves across the Americas of their enslaved origins, but the story of slavery transcends slave origins and is important for many more people than the descendants of slaves themselves. Slavery was a defining institution that helped to transform key areas of the Americas and grievously damaged Africa while enhancing European well-being. In addition, and unlike other, earlier (and later) forms of slavery, slavery in the Americas became a highly racialized institution. The legacy of racial slavery lived on, long after black slavery had been destroyed, through a complex legacy of racial attitudes and discriminations that plagued the west throughout the nineteenth and twentieth centuries. The sins of the fathers continued to plague their descendants, black and white, from the days of plantation slavery to the present day.

Atlantic slavery was only one variant of a myriad species of slavery, but it is Atlantic slavery that springs to mind whenever slavery is discussed, and it has become one of those rare historical phenomena: an institution that, though apparently belonging to a distant past, can fuel a host of current arguments. Most troubling of all, perhaps, the twentieth century confirmed that slavery has remarkable abilities to revive and reinvent itself and to spring back to life when it had seemed dead and gone.

Chronology

1502	First Africans landed in Americas.
1562–63	Sir John Hawkins' first English slave trade voyage.
1607	Settlement of Jamestown, Virginia.
1619	First Africans sold in Jamestown, Virginia.
1632	Establishment of Maryland.
1625–55	British settle their own Caribbean islands.
1640–80	First large-scale African importations into British sugar islands.
1663	Settlement of Carolina. Split into two in 1713.
1730–40	Beginnings of Maroon wars (Cudjoe), Jamaica.
1735–36	Tackey's revolt, Antigua.
1739	Stono's rebellion, South Carolina.
1760	Tackey's revolt, Jamaica.
1776	Society of Friends (Quakers) in England and Pennsylvania requires members to free their slaves.
1777	Constitution of Vermont prohibits slavery.
1780	Pennsylvania adopts policy of gradual emancipation.
1784	Rhode Island and Connecticut pass gradual emancipation.
1787	Foundation of the Society for the Abolition of the Slave Trade.
1789	French Revolution.
1791	Haitian Revolution. Results in foundation of Haitian Republic, 1804.
1792–1815	Revolutionary and Napoleonic Wars. Disruption throughout Atlantic empires.
1794	French National Convention emancipates all slaves in French colonies. Repealed by Napoleon in 1804.
1795–96	Second Maroon War, Jamaica.
1795–97	Fedon's rebellion, Grenada.
1799	New York state passes gradual emancipation.
1800	Gabriel Prosser's revolt, Virginia.
1800	US citizens banned from exporting slaves.
1804	Haitian independence.
1804	New Jersey passes gradual emancipation.
1807	British and Americans outlaw slave trade.
1813	Gradual emancipation adopted in Argentina.
1814	Gradual emancipation adopted in Colombia.
1815	Congress of Vienna. British begin diplomatic campaign to outlaw slave trade.
1816	Bussa's rebellion, Barbados.
1819	British establish Royal Navy anti-slave trade squadron off West Africa.
1822	Denmark Vesey's revolt, South Carolina.
1823	Slave rebellion, Demerara (Guyana).

1823	Slavery abolished in Chile.
1823	Foundation of Anti-Slavery Committee, London.
1825	*Amistad* seized off Long Island.
1829	Slavery abolished in Mexico.
1831	Slavery abolished in Bolivia.
1831	Nat Turner's revolt, Virginia.
1831–32	'Baptist War', Jamaican slave revolt.
1834	Slavery replaced by apprenticeship in British colonies.
1838	Full freedom granted in British colonies.
1841	Quintuple Treaty: Britain, France, Russia, Prussia and Austria agree to suppress slave trade on high seas.
1842	Slavery abolished in Uruguay.
1848–49	Slavery abolished in French and Danish colonies.
1851	Slavery abolished in Ecuador.
1851	Slave trade ended to Brazil.
1854	Slavery abolished in Peru and Venezuela.
1861–65	American Civil War.
1862	Slave trade ended to Cuba.
1863	Slavery abolished in all Dutch colonies.
1865	Thirteenth Amendment abolishes slavery in USA.
1871	Gradual emancipation begun in Brazil.
1873	Slavery abolished in Puerto Rico.
1886	Slavery abolished in Cuba.
1888	Slavery abolished in Brazil.

Further reading

The following titles are offered not for specialists but to provide general readers with a guide to further reading. Those with an asterisk are especially useful.

D. Armitage and M. J. Braddick, *The British Atlantic World*, New York, 2000.
*Ira Berlin, *Many Thousands Gone*, Cambridge, Mass., 1998.
Philip Curtin, *The Rise and Fall of the Plantation Complex*, Cambridge, 1990.
Jonathan Earle, *The Routledge Atlas of American History*, London, 2000.
Jonathan Earle, *The Routledge Atlas of African American History*, London, 2000.
*David Eltis, *The Rise of African Slavery in the Americas*, Cambridge, 2000.
Andrew K. Franks, *The Routledge Historical Atlas of the American South*, London, 1999.
*Greville Freeman-Grenville, *An Atlas of African History*, New York, 1991.
John Iliffe, *Africa: History of a Continent*, Cambridge, 1999.
*Herbert Klein. *The Atlantic Slave Trade*, Cambridge, 1999.
*P. Kolchin, *American Slavery*, London, 1995.
Paul Lovejoy, *Transformations In Slavery*, Cambridge, 2000.
*P. Marshall, ed., *The Oxford History of the British Empire: The Eighteenth Century*, Oxford, 1998.
W. D. Phillips, *Slavery from Roman Times to the Early Atlantic Slave Trade*, Minnesota, 1985.
*Andrew Porter, *An Atlas of British Overseas Expansion*, London, 1991.
A. L. Stinchcombe, *Sugar Island Slavery*, Princeton, 1995.
David Watts, *The West Indies*, Cambridge, 1987.

Index